VIRGINIA
LAND OF MANY DREAMS

First English edition published by Colour Library Books Ltd.
© 1983 Illustrations and text: Colour Library International Ltd.
  99 Park Avenue, New York, N.Y. 10016, U.S.A.
This edition is published by Crescent Books
Distributed by Crown Publishers, Inc.
h g f e d c b a
Colour separations by REPROCOLOR LLOVET, Barcelona, Spain.
Display and text filmsetting by ACESETTERS LTD., Richmond, Surrey, England.
Printed by Cayfosa and bound by Eurobinder - Barcelona (Spain)
ISBN 0.517.414899
CRESCENT 1983

Dep. Leg. B. 2.431/84

VIRGINIA
LAND OF MANY DREAMS

Text by Bill Harris

Produced by
TED SMART and DAVID GIBBON

CRESCENT BOOKS

In a country that prides itself on not having an aristocracy, it is interesting that most Americans casually accept the idea that to be a Virginian is to be an aristocrat. It is even more ironic, considering that many of the ideas Americans have about themselves are ideas that originated in this place, the site of the first permanent English settlement in America.

To be descended from the 'First Families of Virginia' is accepted almost everywhere as an article of faith that one is somehow endowed with some superior quality of breeding and character. With it comes an attitude in the Virginians themselves, a humble but regal air, that makes the idea entirely acceptable.

The earliest settlers first came to Virginia to get rich, by mining gold. In fact, many of them were metalsmiths who had a tough time making a living when they were finally forced to admit there was no gold under the beautiful hills of Virginia.

They may have given up too soon. A vein of gold runs from the Potomac River in Northern Virginia down into Appomattox County. A single mine there produced more than $1.2 million in gold from the time it was opened in 1825 until the beginning of the Civil War. And in those days, the price of gold was a good bit lower than it is today – just about $17 an ounce.

But many others made a very good living indeed from another kind of gold: tobacco. The soil and climate of Virginia are perfect for growing it, and after Sir Walter Raleigh took samples back to London, it didn't take long to get the folks back home addicted to it. It was better than gold! The result was that while other colonies in the New World were establishing cities and getting involved in the problems that go with urban living, Virginia was establishing a society around a plantation system. Being English, they built their farms on the only model they knew: the English manor. With slaves from the West Indies, and indentured servants from England to do the work, each 'farmer' became comparable to an English lord. Each plantation was a self-supporting community, with the owner accepting full responsibility for the lives of everyone. The system thrived for well over two centuries, and the descendants of these 'lords' still, naturally, feel the influence.

The real 'First Families of Virginia' have no descendants at all. In fact, to this day, no one knows what became of them. It's one of the great unsolved mysteries of early America.

The French and Spanish had made attempts at colonizing North America, and British explorers had taken home tales that fired imaginations all over England. But the one imagination that was slow to catch the spark belonged to Queen Elizabeth. The potential profits sounded good to her, but the expense of financing a colony in America didn't seem worth it. Finally, she gave a charter to Sir Humphrey Gilbert and sent him off to find a good spot to settle. On his way back from the trip, with word he couldn't find anywhere good enough, the ship sank and poor Sir Humphrey was drowned.

To help recover her investment, the Queen gave another charter to Gilbert's half brother, Walter Raleigh. Raleigh organized an expedition which set out with two ships and, in 1584, landed on Roanoke Island, along the coast of North Carolina. The Indians were friendly, but very poor. In exchange for some fine iron hatchets, they handed over some deerskins and some dried tobacco leaves. They already had plenty of deerskins in England, and it would have required quite a highly-developed imagination to foresee the value of the tobacco, so Raleigh's expedition captured two of the Indians and took them back home with them.

Tales of the wonderful new land that had been discovered inspired Elizabeth to name the place 'Virginia' in honor of herself – 'the Virgin Queen'. More than that, she made Raleigh a knight and agreed to finance a second expedition.

In 1585, 100 Englishmen, recruited by Sir Walter Raleigh, went back to Roanoke Island and started building a colony. But they were soldiers, not farmers, and things went badly for them. They were forced to depend on the natives for food, but the Indians were too poor for that. In the midst of it all, Sir Francis Drake stopped by on his way home from plundering the Spanish colonies to the south. The struggling colonists took advantage of the opportunity and hitched a ride back home. Soon after, a supply ship arrived from England and, finding the island deserted by the colonists, went back to report to Raleigh what had (or hadn't) been found.

Raleigh's answer to that was to send out a second colonizing expedition. This time, though, many of them decided to take their wives along. Among them was a woman named Eleanor Dare.

Their intention was to move further north this time. But the Portuguese captain who commanded their three ships dropped them at Roanoke Island anyway, and they were stuck with the same problems the earlier colony had faced. But now the problem was compounded. Eleanor Dare had given birth to a child, a girl she named Virginia in honor of the land of her birth. She was the first English child born in the New World, and clearly represented a new problem.

Her grandfather, John White, the leader of the colony, was sent back to England for supplies and help. But by the time he got there, every available ship was being used to defend England against the Spanish Armada, and the fate of the country seemed much more important than that of her colonies. Three years passed before he got back to Virginia, and by then the colony on Roanoke Island was deserted. It had vanished without trace. There was no sign of a struggle, no bodies, nothing disturbed. It was as if everyone had gone off to church and would be back soon. But they never came back. And, to this day, no one knows where they went.

Meanwhile, back in England, things weren't going too well for Sir Walter Raleigh. His failures in Virginia made it just about impossible to raise money for more expeditions. Then Queen Elizabeth died.

The new King, James I, suspected Raleigh of fomenting war with Spain, so he gave him an apartment in the Tower of London and took away his charter for Virginia. Before Raleigh kept his date with the headsman's axe, the King had granted two new charters to colonize North America. The London Company was given the right to settle lands north of Spanish Florida to the Chesapeake Bay, and it was under their charter that three ships arrived in that Bay in April 1607.

One of the 105 colonists aboard didn't see the beautiful flowers, trees and lush countryside as they headed toward the river they would call James in honor of their King. He didn't taste the strawberries one of them described as 'four times bigger and better' than anyone had seen in England. His name was John Smith. He would soon be their leader, even their savior. But in his first moments in the New World, Captain Smith was in irons in the hold of one of the ships.

Before they left England, the King, in his perverse wisdom, had placed the names of the men he wanted to run the colony in a sealed box and had given strict orders that it should not be opened until they arrived in Virginia. Captain John Smith was born to the job and it was apparent to the rest of them right away. Some who fancied themselves the King's choice, however, accused Smith of plotting to kill them and take control for himself as 'King of Virginia'. Because of the force of his personality, the story made enough sense to the others for Smith to be put in custody until the King's wishes were made known.

The box was finally opened, and John Smith was among those named to the ruling council, so he was freed. But his enemies among the others named made sure freedom was all he got, and Smith was denied a voice in running the new colony, which they established at a place they called Jamestown, on the banks of the James River, not far from the home of the King of the Rappahannock Indians, a man they called Powhatan.

Powhatan was the absolute ruler of 20 different tribes in the Chesapeake area, some 8,000 people. Though he seemed to be friendly at first, he didn't like the English intruders. Little by little he made his feelings known, and though the English had the advantage of guns against bows and arrows, they knew they needed help. They found it in the person of Captain John Smith, whom they finally recognized as their obvious leader. His first act was to replace the tent city they called Jamestown with one built of wood and surrounded by a wooden wall. Then he went out to trade with the Indians for food. His early trips were successful, but every time he left Jamestown his enemies there tried to take over again. And if that wasn't enough, the Indians started to turn against him, too.

The Indians got him first.

He was ambushed by one of Powhatan's war parties while exploring a swamp and was taken to the King's court where he was kept as a showpiece for several weeks. When he wasn't being paraded for the entertainment of visiting tribal leaders, the King ordered him to entertain the favorite of his 30 children, a little girl of twelve named Pocahontas.

Smith had been an armorer in his younger days in England, and spent his time in captivity making trinkets and beads for the girl, who, in return, taught him her language and explained many of the customs of her people. She learned English at the same time, and a great friendship grew between the little Indian girl and the soldier of fortune who had earned fame in the civilized world fighting Turks for the Archduke of Austria.

Then, suddenly, Powhatan, apparently bored with the game of showing off his prisoner, ordered Smith brought to trial. The ceremony included a great feast attended by more than 200 of the King's courtiers. Smith's own, third-person account of the event describes the outcome:

'...A long consultation was held, and the conclusion was, two great stones were brought before Powhatan. Then, as many as could layd hands on him (Smith), dragged him to them, and thereon laid his head, and being ready with their clubs to beate out his brains. Pocahontas, the King's dearest daughter, when no entreaty could prevaile, got his head in her arms and laid down her own upon his to save him from death. Whereat the Emperor was content that he should live to make him hatchets and her beads, bells and copper.'

More than that, Powhatan made Smith his adopted son and offered him a principality of his own. But, through the intercession of the Princess, he was allowed to return to Jamestown, where he was made President of the colony.

The colony, though, was starving to death.

Once again, Pocahontas came to the rescue. All through the winter, every four or five days, a train of Indian braves, led by a child with a white heron feather in her raven-black hair, arrived in Jamestown with gifts of corn and game. In that way, they survived the winter and soon grew into a thriving little community of more than 500 people now able to live without fear of Indians.

To cement the peace, King James decreed that Powhatan be crowned officially as Emperor of Virginia. 'A complemental courtesy' was what the King called it. In reality, it was a move to put the Indians under English control by making their ruler a vassal of the Crown. But the old Indian wouldn't go to Jamestown to accept the honor. His own court was good enough for him. And so Smith and his people held the ceremony in the same

place where he had nearly had his brains dashed out only two years before.

New rumours started about Smith's ambitions after that. People said he would marry the Princess and through her become a king. But the rumours stopped abruptly when an injury made it necessary for Captain Smith to go back home to England. He never returned to Virginia again. He did return to America, though. In the employ of the Plymouth Company (holder of the second of the King's charters), he sailed around the Northern coast, presumably studying the possibility of setting up a whaling industry there. The result of his voyage was a book he called *A Description of New England*. It made him even more famous and gave a name to a corner of the United States that has lasted to this day.

He saw Pocahontas again, too. Seven years later, as the wife of an Englishman, John Rolfe, the Princess was presented at the Court of St. James. She died in England of smallpox at the age of twenty-two. Her contribution to the establishment of Virginia was summed up in a tribute by a descendant of another distinguished Virginian, Patrick Henry, who wrote:

'Pocahontas, born the daughter of a savage king, was endowed with all the graces which became a Christian princess. She was the first of her people to embrace Christianity and to unite in marriage with the English race. Like a guardian angel, she watched over and preserved the infant colony which has developed into a great people.'

The time after Smith's departure is called in the history of Jamestown 'the starving time'. It ended when two pinnaces arrived from Bermuda under the command of Sir Thomas Gates, who expected to find a community of 500 people but instead found only 65 creatures he described as 'anatomies'. Regaling him with tales of the horrible winter they had just been through, tales that included hints of cannibalism, they asked him to take them away from Jamestown and burn the place to the ground. He agreed to take them home, and history seemed ready to repeat itself with a second lost colony in Virginia.

But, as the ships were waiting for a wind to take them out to sea, they were intercepted by Lord De la Warr who talked them into turning back and making a fresh start. Turn back they did, and gave the job of making the fresh start work to Lord De la Warr.

He made a hard bargain with them. He ruled with an iron will, often handing out death sentences, and there was a general sigh of relief when he sailed back to England in the spring. He was replaced by an even tougher governor, but the colonists were tough themselves. They survived and even flourished, and before too many years were able to think about taking on the job of governing themselves.

Things began coming together for them in 1619, the year before the Pilgrims arrived at Plymouth Rock up in Massachusetts. In London, Sir Edwin Sandys was made treasurer of the London Company, the controller of Jamestown's destiny. The year before he had drawn up a charter suggesting a representative form of government for the Virginia colony. It allowed settlers to own their own land, to make their own laws, to be treated like Englishmen. Now he had the power to back up his beliefs in spite of the fact that King James had remarked that the document was the work of 'the devile himself'. In the same year, a new governor, Sir George Yeardly, arrived with instructions to change the government in Virginia and news that no less than 11 ships and 1,216 settlers were following him.

Also in the news that year was that 90 young women were on the way 'to make wives for the colonists'. And during the summer, a Dutch man-of-war called with a cargo of African 'immigrants'. Slavery had come to Virginia, though it wouldn't become a legalized institution for another 42 years.

During the same summer, representative government came to Virginia, too. And through it, eventually, to the entire United States.

The new government was run by the General Assembly of Virginia, composed of two groups, one called the councilors, appointed by the London Company and the other, called the burgesses, elected by the freemen of the colony. Modeled on English law, the body not only made laws, but served as a court as well. The Governor had veto power and none of the laws passed by the Assembly were to be considered valid until approved by the London Company. But it was a start, and a good one. The colony was free to grow, and the people, for the first time, had a voice in how it should grow.

From the very start, colonists arrived in Virginia with specific destinations in mind, and most of those destinations were the plantations that were spreading out from along the James River. Each of them was independent from all the others and only loosely associated with the colony at Jamestown. It shocked people like William Bradford up in Plymouth, who complained that each was 'a distinct body by themselves under the general Government'. But it worked well enough for the Virginians, and representatives of no less than seven private plantations were part of the original House of Burgesses.

The idea of importing wives for the settlers originated in London. The Company knew that 'the planters' mindes may be faster tied to Virginia' if they had wives to keep those minds occupied. Accordingly, they sent a ship with 'younge, handsome and honestly educated maydes, especially recommended unto the Companie for their good bringinge up'. The Governor was given orders to place them into the homes of good families and to watch over their welfare until such time as they 'happened upon good matches'. They were not to be turned into servants, nor forced into a marriage they didn't want.

Naturally, the girls didn't have any problem at all finding husbands. In fact, the Assembly was forced to pass a law that prohibited them from being engaged to more than one man at a time.

In addition to the women, about 100 children from the streets of London were sent to Virginia to seek their fortunes. Many families arrived as well. In 1619, almost 1,300 people arrived in Virginia, doubling the size of the colony. And to end the year on an up-beat note, Parliament passed a law forbidding the planting of tobacco in either England or Ireland. A banner year indeed!

By 1622, only 1,000 of the 14,000 colonists who had emigrated to Virginia had lived to tell about it. No disaster in the history of the world, from the longest war to the grimmest plague, has ever taken the lives of such a large proportion of a population in so short a space of time. Through it all they never lost faith in the future. This was their home now, for better or for worse. They had turned their backs on the old country once and for all.

But Virginia wasn't out of the woods yet.

When the Indian Emperor Powhatan died in 1618, the new leader, Opechancanough, reassured the white men that peace between them was so firm that the sky would fall before it would end. The sky fell on the morning of Good Friday, March 22, 1622. In a well-planned campaign, bands of Indian braves attacked some 80 settlements on both sides of the James River at exactly the same hour. More than 350 colonists were killed and a new Indian war begun. The attack came almost without warning. Jamestown and the settlements near it were spared because an Indian boy named Chanco, who was a well-treated servant in the home of a settler, warned the white man that he had been asked to kill him. The settler rushed to Jamestown to warn the Governor, and their defenses were in place before the attack came.

The Indians took no prisoners except about two dozen women who remained their captives for more than a year.

With hostile Indians wandering around the countryside, it seemed like a good idea to move the people away from the plantations into the towns. It may have saved their lives, but it made life harder. Overcrowding led to disease, farmers weren't able to get any corn planted, livestock had been driven off and the men were too busy with sentry duty to do anything else.

They turned to London for help, but they might have well have asked the Indians to help them. Officials of the London Company were furious. These Virginians were no better than naughty children, they said. London had warned them time and again that tobacco was just a passing fad, yet they continued defiantly to grow it. Why didn't they grow more corn so they could feed themselves? Their whole purpose in America, said London, was 'to improve the Companie's revenues, not depleat the treasury with frivolous requests for supplies'. Furthermore, if they didn't get their act together, the Virginians would find themselves 'clean left and abandoned'. And they'd better get busy, the Company added, because new colonists were already on the way.

More than 1,000 arrived that summer.

The ships they came in had supplies, though not much, and they also brought a new disease, which many believe might have been the plague. One colonist said the new immigrants had been 'poisoned with stinkage beer, all falling sick and spreading the contagion'. During the winter twice as many died as had been massacred by the Indians.

Each ship brought new orders from London, too, but they were usually the same as the old ones: 'work hard, go to church, send money and quit complaining'.

But the complaints were being heard all over England. King James finally stepped in, and among other things, ordered that the Company's stockholders, who were themselves grumbling over never having collected a dividend, should be assessed to help save the colony from starvation. He also ordered a reorganization of the Company. When they dragged their feet, the King organized an investigative commission and before long was able to revoke the Company's charter and take control of the colony himself.

King James was not one of the world's great believers in representative government, and Virginians began to worry about what would become of their House of Burgesses. But they didn't fret long because James died within a few months of taking over. His son, Charles I, was a chip off the old block, but Parliament was giving him a hard time and he didn't pay much attention to what was going on across the Atlantic. In answer to their petitions, he allowed them to hold an election in 1628 and another the following year. After that, they didn't bother to ask, but went on having elections anyway. Ten years later, Charles made it official by agreeing that no laws or taxes could be imposed without the approval of the House of Burgesses. The King appointed the Governor, who, in his name, appointed the Council. Colonists served on the Council, and that effectively limited the King's power. For the first time the pattern was established that the British colonies in America were to be self-governing. It was a pattern a future king would regret.

The Indians had quietened a great deal, and the colony began growing outward. Planters had discovered that they could get three consecutive crops of tobacco from a field before the soil nutrients dried up. It was still good for growing corn, but the real profits were in tobacco, and the obvious answer was to clear new fields every three years. In the process, some of the plantations became enormous. To help work the fields, they imported indentured servants from England. In return for their passage and a place to live when they got to Virginia, these people, many from poorhouses and jails, many of them children, agreed to work for their benefactor for a specified length of time, during which they were housed, clothed and fed, but not paid. At the end of the contract period, they were given 'freedom dues', a piece of land, possibly a set of tools or even money. As part of the agreement, many were taught to read and write and some were taught a trade.

By 1635, the Colony was growing enough food to feed itself and even to export corn to the new colony up in Massachusetts. And with the new prosperity a new breed of Virginian began to emerge; the aristocracy. Back home in England, you could tell an aristocrat by, among other things, the amount of land he owned. Here in Virginia, everyone believed that the more land you could acquire the higher you sat in the social structure. No matter that there was plenty of land for everyone, it was, to their English minds, a symbol of power and wealth. The idea had been given an official stamp by the London Company who had given estates to people in authority. It was cheaper than paying them, but that's a point almost everyone seems to have missed.

In the early days of the colony, people settled in towns because it was safer, and it was the pattern they were used to in England. But as land fever spread so did the population, and isolated farms were home to many more Virginians than were cities and towns. Though Jamestown was still the capital, a huge number of people lived several days journey from it, and that made the government a little less representative than it seemed on paper. To solve the problem, the colony was divided into counties and, in each, a government representative was authorized to hold court once a month to settle minor disputes. Courthouses were eventually built at convenient locations, often where there was no town at all. The justice of the peace was an ordinary citizen, probably with no legal training, who used 'horse sense' in making decisions. He was also charged with enforcing local laws ranging from the price of a mug of ale in the county's taverns to issuing marriage licenses.

The church was an important institution too. From the very beginning there were laws that made worship compulsory. Anyone who didn't show up was fined a pound of tobacco. If you didn't appear for a month of Sundays, the fine was 50 pounds of tobacco. As people moved out into the countryside, the rule was tougher to obey. In some areas chapels were served by circuit-riding preachers; in others, big landowners had chapels in their homes.

In the days of the London Company, the Bishop of London managed the church's affairs in Virginia. But under the new rules, it was up to the King to appoint a bishop for them, and that was a detail he never got around to. Virginians considered themselves members of the Church of England, and didn't take kindly to any other religion. Without an English bishop, though, they began to adapt the old church into something new and slightly different.

In England, the bishop appointed the minister for each parish, and only he could remove them. In Virginia, each parish elected 12 men to serve as a vestry, and they were the ones who picked the preacher. A great many people in search of social status called themselves ministers, so the job wasn't as simple as it seemed. When the bishop was doing the hiring, the minister had a job for life. Virginia vestries hired their clergymen for one-year terms. If he worked out and everyone agreed, the Governor made the job a permanent one, and then only he could remove him.

To help give the vestries authority, the General Assembly added a law to the books that warned, 'ministers shall not give themselves to excess in drinking or riot, spending their time idly by day or by night, playing at dice, cards or any other unlawful game'.

Churches were the center of social activity in Colonial times, and very important in keeping track of the morals of the people. The physical distance between the people and the central government made the church's job that much more important, and that made members of the vestries very powerful indeed.

They controlled church property and funds, they collected tithes to help the needy, then decided who the needy were. From their number, they elected two wardens, whose job it was to keep their eyes peeled for examples of '...scandalous offenses, such as dishonest company-keeping with women and other enormous sins'.

Since many families were led by men who were at the same time justices of the peace and church vestrymen, some began to dominate the life of the colony. Power was passed from fathers to sons, and the 'first families of Virginia' became a factor to deal with.

It was easy to tell who was important. The men often wore big lace collars and broad-brimmed hats. Their shoes had buckles made of silver, the swords at their sides dangled from gold belts. They sometimes had a lock of hair curled fetchingly over one ear and tied with a bit of ribbon belonging to their lady-love. Their ladies wore hoop skirts or silk and satin gowns, their ears were weighed down with diamonds and they were practically round-shouldered from the weight of the pearls around their necks.

They entertained a great deal, and were proud of the fact that, unlike their English counterparts, they let almost anyone eat at their tables and sleep in their homes. They served wine imported from Europe or beer they brewed themselves. Their tables groaned with venison, turkey and quail. As long as lesser Virginians knew their place, life was nothing short of perfect.

The Indian threat, like the days of starvation, was a dim memory, and the only talk of it was a constantly repeated rumor that old Opechancanough had finally been dispatched to the happy hunting ground. But that was not the case.

Back home in England, things weren't going well for King Charles. He had come to blows with Parliament over who had the most power and he had to contend with the Puritans who were very unhappy with the state of the Church of England. Virginians generally sided with the King because he had already given them the rights Parliament was fighting for and because they were quite content with the state of the Church of England. They were also pleased with the man Charles had sent to be their Governor, Sir William Berkeley.

Though Berkeley kept Virginia neutral, the war reached the James River in 1644 when a ship flying the royal colors was attacked by two others under the Parliament flag. It all happened quickly, and with little damage. But deep in the forest, Opechancanough's braves watched with great interest.

For more than two decades, the old Indian had been waiting and watching for an opportunity to push the hated English off his lands. Even though it was reported 'his sinews had slackened, and his eyelids had become so heavy he could not see but as they were lifted up by his servants', his hate was as strong as ever.

The gunfire on the river was a signal, he thought, that the English were finally fighting among themselves. And that was his signal to attack. Nearly 500 people died in the massacre, mostly in frontier settlements. Jamestown was too well-fortified, and, quite simply, there were too many white men in Virginia to drive away.

Berkeley and the Council reacted quickly and began building a string of forts along the main rivers. Then, after two years of fighting, they captured the old Indian chief, who many (probably accurately) said was 100 years old. Berkeley had an idea that he would make a gift of the Indian to the King. It would, he thought, be a living testament that Virginia was a place where a man could live a healthy, long life. He might have done it, too, but one of Opechancanough's braves, outraged by the indignity, shot the old chief in the back.

The Indian problem was finally settled with a treaty that, among other things, forced the natives to pay tribute to the white men at the time the wild geese flew south each year. Today, Indians who live in Virginia still pay the tribute every year when they present a Thanksgiving turkey to the Governor.

The same year the treaty was signed, across the Atlantic, Oliver Cromwell and his Parliamentary allies consigned the King to prison. When he was beheaded three years later, the Virginia Assembly proclaimed his son, Charles II, to be his successor. No matter that it would be another 11 years before England agreed, in Virginia it was treason to think otherwise.

People who had fought against Cromwell in the civil wars were known as 'Cavaliers'. Many were English peers, quite a few were not. No matter what their status, Berkeley assured them they'd find a warm welcome, and a haven, in Virginia.

People with names like Randolph and Carter, Lee and Mason, whose descendants meant so much to the history of both Virginia and America, answered the call.

When Cromwell died and the monarchy was restored, King Charles II obviously had a warm place in his heart for his colony in Virginia. He referred to it by a name that's still used today, the 'Old Dominion'. Then his enthusiasm went too far. As a reward to some influential people who had stood by him during the unpleasantness, he created a new colony for them and named it 'Carolina' in his own honor.

A nice gesture, to be sure. Except the land he granted had been part of Virginia until then, and that made a lot of Virginians a lot less loyal to the Crown.

Then, to add insult to injury, English laws were changed to take some of the profitability out of the Virginia tobacco business.

Things were tough, but so were the Virginians, and many pushed west in search of new fortunes in the fur business. Governor Berkeley granted licenses to them to trade with the Indians, but his power over the red men didn't extend to the western tribes. Naturally there was trouble on the frontier, and settlers blamed the Governor. Added to the depression back East and anger at the King, the Indian problem made Virginia a powder keg waiting for someone to light the fuse.

The man with the match was 29-year-old Nathaniel Bacon, who had been sent to America from England by his father as punishment for marrying the wrong woman. Within a year of arriving in Virginia, he became a member of the Colonial Council. Within two years, he became the leader of the first American revolution.

In the early spring of 1676, Indians attacked Bacon's plantation and killed his overseer. He asked the Governor for permission to form his own militia and go off on a retaliatory raid. The Governor didn't answer his letter, so Bacon's own answer was to lead 70 of his neighbors into the interior. 'If the redskins meddle with me', he said, 'I'll harry them, commission or no commission!'

He headed south in search of the Susquehannock tribe who had been causing most of the trouble. His idea was to wipe out the tribe completely, and to make the plan work, he enlisted another tribe, the Occaneechi, to help him. When the job was done, he turned on the Occaneechi, burned their village and sent them packing.

When he got back, the Governor had suspended him from the Council and condemned him as a rebel. But Bacon had the people on his side. When they unanimously elected Bacon a burgess, Berkeley had him arrested and forced him to make a public apology. And that, thought the governor, was that.

The Governor was wrong. The truce lasted a short time until Bacon began hearing rumors that he was about to be murdered. That was enough to make him leave town, and when he did, the Governor once more branded him a traitor and issued a warrant for his arrest. In answer to that, Bacon rounded up 250 rebels like himself and marched on Jamestown. He led them right up to the door of the statehouse and demanded to see the Governor.

Berkeley challenged him to a duel, but the younger man refused, demanding instead the commission to fight Indians that he had asked for a few weeks before. By morning, he had his commission as well as a pardon and a personal letter to the King excusing him. Then he took his men and went off to fight some Indians.

No sooner had he gone than Berkeley revoked the commission and publicly branded Bacon a traitor for the third time. Then he got word that Bacon was on the way back, and was not exactly in the mood for friendly discussion.

By the time Bacon got to Jamestown, Berkeley was across the bay on the Eastern Shore and the young rebel found himself in charge of the rest of Virginia.

He knew the King would send troops to end his defiance, but he set up a new government anyway and asked the people for their loyalty not only against the Indians, but against England herself. It was an odd concept for them, but they agreed.

Yet another time he took off to find Indians, and once again Berkeley went back to Jamestown, this time with an army to defend it. As it turned out, the army was staffed by men who admired Bacon's style and the best the Governor could do was to retreat to ships in the harbor when the rebels got back. The ships were armed, and Bacon's enthusiasm was no match for cannons. Realizing he couldn't hold the town, he ordered it burned to the ground. Then he retreated to the Governor's home outside the town and issued a declaration of independence calling on Virginians to defend their rights or give up their colony. His next step was to make a grand tour to drum up support. He hadn't gone far when he contracted a fever and died before the King could rule on his leadership.

On hearing of Bacon's death, the Governor took charge again, and, without their leader, the rebels were no match for him. He hanged 20 of them on the spot without a trial. 'More than I have hanged for the murder of my father', said King Charles. To put an end to it, the King sent a new Governor to Virginia, but old Berkeley refused to accept the fact he'd been fired. It took five months to convince him he should go to London to explain himself, but by that time he was too old and sick to stand trial.

He died without ever realizing that he had allowed Bacon to start a fire in America that would smolder for the next hundred years.

The Governors who followed Berkeley were an unimpressive lot and included Lord Culpeper, who asked the King to raise his salary from $50,000 to $100,000 a year and pay for it with an export tax on tobacco. When the Assembly gave him an argument, he snorted, 'If this continues, it will make the exercise of assemblies wholly impractical, if not impossible'. Next he proceeded to order that the burgesses could do nothing without the King's specific permission. Then, declaring Jamestown dull and depressing, even though it had been newly rebuilt, he loaded his entourage into a ship and sailed home to England.

The King ordered him back to put an end to rioting over the low price of tobacco, but he was more bored than ever and stayed only a month or two before going home again, where he was fired and stripped of all his property except 5,000,000 acres, which, some years later gave to a young surveyor named George Washington his first job.

Toward the end of the 17th century, the short reign of James II ended and things began to look better for both Englishmen and Virginians, with William and Mary on the throne.

Slavery had been legalized in Virginia some years before, and big planters were beginning to import blacks to help them produce more tobacco. Trouble in France made it necessary for Huguenots to look for a better place to live, and they found a perfect place in Virginia. Scotland and Ireland had long since found Virginia a convenient place to dump political prisoners, but now Scots and Irishmen were beginning to come on their own. English Quakers moved south from Pennsylvania along with Welsh Baptists, bringing a challenge to Virginia's Anglicans. And German immigrants began clearing farms in the Piedmont. For the first time, Virginia was less an outpost of the British Empire than a self-sufficient colony with a personality all its own.

The great estates in the Tidewater boasted Georgian houses that were the envy of all America, and their owners lived as much like the landed gentry in England as they possibly could. Further west in the Piedmont, houses were smaller and more fortress-like, and their owners more likely to be small farmers than rich planters. Many built mills and factories, too, and hard work was almost a religion.

In Virginia, as in the other American colonies, a shortage of good preachers was a worrisome thing. The answer was to establish colleges to educate them. An emissary was sent to London to secure a charter in the interest of saving souls in the colony. After having been told, 'damn your souls! Make tobacco!' (it was by then England's biggest revenue-producer) the charter was granted and a few years later, the College of William and Mary sputtered into life in a temporary building with a staff of three including a president, a writing master and an 'usher'. When it finally got a building of its own, it was a place called 'Middle Plantation' a few miles inland from Jamestown. The building itself was designed by the great Sir Christopher Wren who reported that his plan had been 'adapted to the nature of the country by the gentlemen there'. In spite of the apparent tampering by a committee, the building was among the most magnificent in the British Empire. In the years since, it has survived the 'improvements' of later architects as well as two major fires and stands today restored to its original lines. It's still one of the great buildings of the world.

At about the same time the College of William and Mary was beginning to establish itself as the cultural center of the colonists, Virginians began to realize that Jamestown had outlived its usefulness as a capital. In 1699, the Assembly ordered it moved to the site of the college and decreed that the name of the new city should be Williamsburg in honor of the King. Privately-owned buildings already on the 300-acre site would be bought and torn down to allow for a planned city that promised to be better than anything in America and even England itself.

It was intended to resemble a 'good country town in England', and succeeded very well indeed. On the orders of the new Governor, Francis Nicholson, every house lot had to be at least a half-acre to allow space for a house, a garden and an orchard. His order specified how far from the street a house could be, and even mandated the height of ceilings. In these days of suburban zoning, such regulations don't seem at all unusual, but in 1699 they surely must have raised a lot of eyebrows, especially in a place like Virginia, where the idea of freedom was as important as life itself.

The Governor said the city should have a broad main street beginning at the new college and running east for a mile to the site of the Capitol. The avenue, which he called Duke of Gloucester Street, would be nine poles, or 90 feet wide. Halfway along its length would be a market square and at right angles to it, another wide avenue reaching toward the Governor's home, which would, after it was built, be called a 'palace'.

Governor Nicholson never lived in the palace. He had earned himself a reputation as a tyrant by threatening to hang 'with the Magna Carta around their necks', any Virginians who thought they deserved the rights of Englishmen. Eventually his reputation reached London and he was recalled. But though he was universally despised in America, his ideas made sense when he talked about Williamsburg, and he had already proven his theories could work by building a city in Maryland called Annapolis.

He had a great sense of politics. After naming the new capital for the King, he proposed a design for its streets that would be a monogram of the letters 'W' and 'M' in honor of the King and Queen. No one dared tell him that streets in that pattern would drop into ravines, force the draining of streams and result in no end of confusion. But, fortunately, he figured it out for himself and opted for a plan that was very much like one that had been proposed more than 30 years before by Sir Christopher Wren for the rebuilding of London after the Great Fire.

Lacking a monogram, he decided to honor the monarchs in the names of the streets. The main street was named for the Queen's son, the Duke of Glouces-ter; another was named for Prince George, husband of Princess Anne, and Nassau Street honored King William's ancestral family. Then, as if to prove he was no mere sycophant, he named the parallel street south of the main one Francis, and the one to the north, Nicholson.

His successor, a man with the unfortunate name of Nott, left his name on a tombstone in Bruton Chur-chyard and not much else.

Williamsburg began to become an important city in 1710 with the arrival of a former hero of the Battle of Blenheim, a young man named Alexander Spotswood.

He was appalled at the condition of Nicholson's model city. The Capitol building had been built (with Nichol-son's coat of arms painted on the cupola!), and was open for business twice a year for 'Publick Times', when the Assembly was meeting and courts were in session. The College building had been severely dam-aged by fire and reconstruction was lagging. The main street was still just a dirt cowpath; the church was falling apart, and worst of all to this young aristocrat, the Governor's residence hadn't even been started.

He went to work to change all that and added orders to build a powder magazine while they were at it. He may have felt he would need protection because, as his crowning effort, he began work on the Governor's residence, which became quite the best house in the colony and was so expensive that the colonists called it 'The Palace'.

It was an impressive effort, and in less than ten years Williamsburg was a place to be proud of. Not more than 2,000 people, slaves and all, ever lived there at any one time and, except in 'Publick Times', it was a quiet country town. When the government came to life, so did the town, and the population usually doubled. Many wealthy planters had townhouses there, and used them for lavish entertaining and politicking. The not-so-rich had to stay in the taverns, five and six to a room. If they didn't like their roommates, they could stay up all night drinking, and gambling at cards and dice.

In the evenings when the Assembly was is session, America's first theater presented productions of Shakespeare's plays performed by actors imported from London. The less sophisticated watched cock-fights and puppet shows, got out of breath in dance contests, or gasped at fireworks displays presented by the Governor himself.

They were essentially country people, and back home in England they were thought of as 'colonials'. But that was among Englishmen who hadn't visited Virginia. One who did was amazed to report that they '...dress after the same modes and behave themselves exactly as the gentry of London'. It would turn out in just a few short years that all England would change its opinion of Americans, and a lot of the change came directly from this little town in Virginia.

What happened there happened in the short space of 60 years. When Thomas Jefferson was elected Governor in 1779, Lord Cornwallis and his English troops had already passed through the town and demonstrated how vulnerable it could be. As a safety measure, Jefferson asked that the Capital be moved to Richmond. When it was done a year later, Williamsburg became just another unimportant country town, and it stayed that way until 1903 when the Rev. Dr. W. A. R. Goodwin accepted a call to become rector of Williamsburg's Bruton Parish Church. He was a native Virginian, fascinated by the state's historic buildings and dismayed by the way they were being allowed to decay. In Williamsburg he had both the best of the old buildings and the best examples of neglect. He also had very little money, but more than made up for it in energy and passion.

Anyone needing the clergyman's services late at night could usually find him with his nose buried in town or church records for clues about what the town may have looked like. If you had a dollar to spare, he'd most likely look you up to ask you to contribute it to the restoration of his church.

Four years after he arrived, he celebrated the 300th anniversary of the establishment of the Episcopal Church in America by rededicating Bruton, restored to look exactly as it had when Governor Spotswood had it spruced up almost 200 years earlier. Everyone in town agreed it was a wonderful thing, but not so wonderful that any of them thought of restoring the whole town. When their rector moved on to Rochester, New York, in 1909, Williamsburgers went back to sleep.

Some of them began to stir again when Dr. Goodwin came back in 1923 to join the faculty at William and Mary. Fortunately, his dream of restoring the town was still very much alive. Then, just as fortunately, he was asked to go to New York to represent the College at a meeting of the Phi Beta Kappa fraternity, an institution that had been founded at William and Mary.

He met John D. Rockefeller, Jr. there, and couldn't resist telling him about his dream. Two years later, Rockefeller arrived in Williamsburg with his wife and four of his sons, Nelson, David, Lawrence and Winthrop, and Dr. Goodwin took them on a walking tour of the little college town. There were about 85 colonial buildings still standing in 1926, including the restored church, which by then had Dr. Goodwin as its rector again.

Rockefeller didn't make any promises, but asked his host to work up a restoration plan and present it to him with a price tag. By the end of 1927, Dr. Goodwin had authorization to begin buying Williamsburg. To keep the identity of his benefactor a secret, he told anyone who asked that the money came from 'Mr. David', a name he concocted after Rockefeller sent him a letter signed 'David's Father'.

Naturally, no matter whose money it was, everyone in town knew their rector wasn't using his own, and before long prices for run-down property began to skyrocket. But he kept buying anyway, all the while keeping the source of the money a deep secret. Then when the time came to transfer title of all the properties, someone in town found a law on the books forbidding the sale of property to unknown persons.

In June, 1928, Dr. Goodwin called a special town meeting in the Williamsburg High School auditorium to tell his eager neighbors:

'About a year ago, Mr. John D. Rockefeller came to Williamsburg...'

He didn't have to tell them much else. They were all quick to agree that the combination of Rockefeller's money and Dr. Goodwin's enthusiasm was the best thing that had happened to their town since Governor Nicholson gave up the idea of having its streets laid out in the form of a William and Mary monogram.

On February 24, 1934, less than six years and more that $12 million later, the Virginia Assembly crowded itself into the Capitol at Williamsburg for the first time in more than 150 years and officially welcomed the past back to Virginia.

The building they met in isn't the original, but it would probably fool any of the original settlers. The old Capitol had long since disappeared and so had most records of what it looked like. After two years of research that took architects as far afield as the Bodleian Library at Oxford, England, the new building was built on the foundations of the old. The designs were carefully detailed to reproduce cornices and brickwork, plastering and hardware as close to 18th-century standards as possible. They used materials from original sources, too, including quarry tiles imported from England for the floors.

There are subtle differences, too. The original building burned down twice, the copy is fireproof. And, of course, the whole place is wired for electricity, a touch that would have amazed even the most imaginative and far-sighted of the original burgesses.

The Williamsburg restoration is one of the most ambitious architectural projects of the 20th century. It's had its detractors of course: Thomas Jefferson called the architecture of the original 'worse than in any other part of America'; Frank Lloyd Wright, the architect, said the restoration shows 'how narrow, how shallow life was in Colonial days'. But millions have walked its streets and taken away ideas that have changed the streets of towns all over the country. It created a national interest in 'recycling' rather than destroying old buildings. And all of the interest in 'Early American' art and architecture comes directly from this restoration. The interest is so strong, the Keeper of the National Register of Historic Places has said that Williamsburg is the 'formulator of popular 20th century taste' in America.

Nothing could be more appropriate. In its relatively short life as capital of Virginia, Williamsburg became almost the formulator of America itself.

It was the place where some of the earliest ideas of westward expansion began. When Governor Spotswood arrived there, one of his first ambitions after he got the city whipped into shape was to see how big the colony could grow. In 1716, he got together a group of 'pioneers and gentlemen' and set out to explore the Shenandoah Valley. When they crossed the Blue Ridge Mountains, they climbed to the top of the highest peak they could find and scratched the name of the King in a rock. It may be one of the earliest examples of graffiti in the history of America. Then they sat down and drank a round of toasts to the King's health and stuck the empty champagne bottles into the ground as a sign that this mountain, which they called Mount George, was the property of the Crown. Another historic moment. Littering had reached the Land of the Free.

The expedition was also one of the earliest to use horseshoes in America. Softer soil and the lack of stones made them unnecessary in the coastal colonies. When they got back, the Governor presented each of his fellow explorers with a horseshoe made of gold and blessed them with the title 'Knights of The Golden Horseshoe'. It was a very select group, and anyone who wanted to join them had to prove he had drunk His Majesty's health at the summit of Mount George, and, presumably, left the bottle behind. In a colony where social-climbing was a fine art, it was a brilliant way to encourage western expansion, and before long English and Scots-Irish settlers were pouring across the mountains from the East and Germans began coming down from the North.

They were a new breed, quite different from the Tidewater planters, and they substituted buckskin for velvet and long rifles and scalping knives for ceremonial swords. The Indians weren't too happy to see their best hunting ground turned into farms. They had named it Shenandoah, 'Daughter of the Stars', and now the stars were falling. They didn't give up without a fight.

But it was a losing fight. These were people who thrived on hardship. People like 'Mad Ann' Baily, whose husband was scalped by Indians, driving her to a life-long search for Indians to scalp in return. She had a good collection of scalps on her belt and a reputation for toughness that was the envy of men who routinely faced grizzly bears and wolves and panthers they swore were the biggest in creation.

Meanwhile, back in Williamsburg, where civilization had long since become established and safe, they faced a more 'civilized' menace: pirates. Piracy was a big business as well as a great adventure in the early 18th century, especially in the West Indies. Not many came as far north as Virginia, but one who did was Captain Teach, who called himself 'Blackbeard'. People said he looked like the Devil himself, and Blackbeard went to a lot of trouble to nurture the image. He braided his long black beard and looped it in strange ways. When he attacked a ship, he put lighted fuses under his hat so smoke would come out around his ears and make him look more terrifying.

He made a deal with the Governor of North Carolina for safety in exchange for half his loot. The Governor's constituents didn't like that much, and turned to Virginia's Governor Spotswood for help. His answer was to send out two ships to take the pirate dead or alive. They took him dead.

The ships sailed back to Virginia with Blackbeard's head on the bowsprit of one and the 13 survivors of his crew in the hold of the other.

By the time Spotswood retired, the colony was safe, happy and prosperous. One of his successors, William Gooch, bragged that 'the ladies and gentlemen here are well bred, not an ill dancer in my government'.

They included men like Robert Carter of Corotoman, who had held every important office in the colony from vestryman to acting Governor. His plantation covered 300,000 acres and was worked by a thousand slaves. Another of the well-bred gentlemen was William Byrd II, the son of a man who had established an Indian trading post near the present site of Richmond back in 1670. The first William Byrd was a frontiersman who spent more than 30 years in the wilderness trading cloth and kettles for furs and herbs. His son spent 30 years of his life in Europe getting a classical education and absorbing the culture that was considered so important back home in Virginia. He could read six languages and had a library that was bigger than any in America except for Cotton Mather's up in Boston. He was a lawyer by profession, and one of the first great American writers. He set standards of style that moved Colonial culture forward to a point that made Americans begin to realize they weren't 'Colonials' any more.

Out West, the French, who considered the territory theirs, told the Indians that the English were robbing them of their country and then joined in the fight to stop the expansion that Virginians were threatening to take all the way to the Ohio River. Even Indians who had been friendly went on the warpath, and the Virginia Government was forced to send in the militia to protect its interests. In charge of the Southern District was a young major who was the grandson of one of the greatest Indian fighters in the history of Virginia. He was 21 years old, with no college educa-

tion and no actual military experience. He was a remarkable man named George Washington.

The French were building a string of forts across territory the English considered theirs, and Washington was picked to deliver a letter of protest, and while he was at it, to have a look around. His report prompted the burgesses to come across with enough money to finance a small army and put Washington in charge of it.

The expedition was a disaster, and after Washington was forced to surrender, England had to send two regiments to take care of the French. That was a disaster, too. They were ambushed and sent packing, and it began to look very much like the territory west of the Blue Ridge would be forever French.

It may well have turned out that way if men like George Washington had been less determined.

The French and the Indians made life on the frontier tougher than it should have been, and Washington's troops were spread too thin to do much about it. Finally the English decided enough was enough and sent troops to drive the French out of the entire continent. When word of that adventure reached Williamsburg, the Assembly got serious about supporting Washington and before long he had men and supplies enough to go on the offensive.

In the winter of 1758, the Virginia militia attacked Fort Duquesne, took it and changed its name to Fort Pitt in honor of the King's First Minister, William Pitt. It had been Pitt's idea to get serious about defending the American colonies, and English troops were at that moment pushing the French back to the north. For the Virginia colony, the fall of Fort Duquesne was enough, and once that was done, Washington, now a colonel, resigned from the military so he could get involved in politics. He was 23 years old and one of the most popular men in Virginia. So popular, in fact, that he had already been elected to the House of Burgesses without campaigning for a single vote. He had influential friends who did the campaigning for him. They also kept track of the expenses, which included £39-6s for rum to get the 794 citizens who voted in the mood to cast their vote the right way. One historian has estimated that the outlay would have bought one and a half quarts for each one of them.

He probably could have saved his money. Everything was going right for him. The preceding spring he had met a young widow with a tidy fortune. He had already inherited a fortune of his own and an estate at Mount Vernon, and with his place in history already secure, he married the widow and settled down to the quiet life of a country gentleman.

One of the men who served under him on the frontier wrote:

'...Judge then how sensibly we must be affected by the loss of such an excellent commander, such a sincere friend and so affable a companion. How rare it is to find those amiable qualifications blended together in one man.'

Of course, the man wasn't lost forever.

Expansion in the West brought a new breed of man into the House of Burgesses and the representatives of the new families didn't get along with the first families. One of the newcomers was a young lawyer named Patrick Henry.

In 1758, the Assembly changed the law to allow clergymen to be paid in cash rather than in tobacco as had been the custom from the beginning. The ministers didn't like that at all, preferring to take their chances on increasing tobacco prices. They brought pressure on London to nullify the law, then sued the Virginia Government for back pay. Patrick Henry was the lawyer selected by the tax collectors.

Some years later, Thomas Jefferson credited him with being able to deliver 'torrents of sublime eloquence'. In the 1763 trial, his opening salvo against the ministers set all Virginia on its ear. 'These rapacious harpies would, were their power equal to their will', he shouted, 'snatch from the hearth of their honest parishioner his last hoe-cake, from the widow and her orphaned children their last milch-cow, the last bed, nay the last blanket from the lying-in woman!'

He accused the King of being a tyrant and said that he had no right to the obedience of his subjects. The jury took less than 5 minutes to cut the award for damages in half. The ministers and others in the courtroom were shocked almost speechless by this young upstart who not only said nasty things about the clergy, but dared to insult the King himself. It was treason pure and simple. The judge in the case later said that the young lawyer told him privately that he had said those things 'to render himself popular'. To which the judge added, somewhat huffily,'...In this person's opinion, the ready road to popularity here is to trample under foot the interests of religion, the rights of the church and the prerogatives of the Crown'.

He hadn't seen anything yet!

Within two years, Patrick Henry had rendered himself popular enough to be elected to the House of Burgesses. And one of his first acts was to win an appointment to a committee charged with examining a new tax England had imposed requiring stamps to be bought and affixed to every type of document, from contracts to advertisements in newspapers, even including playing cards and diplomas. Nobody liked the tax much anywhere in America, but nowhere in America did the Crown have an enemy as eloquent as Patrick Henry.

The series of resolutions he drew up ended with a strong statement that only the General Assembly had a right to impose taxes and any attempt to change the principle '...has a manifest tendency to destroy British as well as American freedom'. The aristocrats in the Assembly thought that smacked of treason and were quick to say so. In the debate that followed, Henry summed up by saying: '...Caesar had his Brutus, Charles the First his Cromwell, and George the Third...'

At that point the Chairman of the Assembly leaped to his feet. Pointing an accusing finger at the freshman burgess, he shouted 'treason!' with all the strength he could muster.

But Patrick Henry scarcely missed a beat. '...And George the Third', he said, 'may profit by their example. If this be treason, make the most of it!'

The Assembly was badly split, but the resolutions carried by one vote. Revolution was in the air in America.

They reconsidered their decision the following day and voted to drop the resolutions because they had been passed in moments of 'rash heat'. But they were a day too late. The text had been printed in newspapers up and down the coast and people were already beginning to hang stamp distributors in effigy.

Up in Massachusetts, leaders had already proposed a general meeting of all the colonies to consider opposition to the stamp taxes, but nobody listened until they heard the news of the 'Virginia Resolves'. Virginia, after all, was the most loyal of all the King's American colonies. If they were willing to stick their necks out, people reasoned, everybody should get behind them.

Within a few months, in October, 1765, representatives of nine colonies met in New York and passed a resolution to boycott British imports until the taxes were removed. Ironically, Virginia was not one of the nine.

Early the following year the stamp taxes were removed and everybody relaxed again. Virginians in particular were the most pleased. Most of the leaders were fiercely loyal to the Crown and were appalled at the idea of opposing 'Good King George'. With this particular thorn removed, they were sure their world would soon get back to normal.

But something had been started in Williamsburg that wouldn't go away that easily.

In 1767, Britain's Chancellor of the Exchequer, Charles Townshend, the man they called 'Champagne Charlie', hit upon an idea that could let him cut taxes at home without any loss to the treasury. He put import taxes on glass, lead, tea, paint and paper to be paid by the American colonies. He told the Americans that the money would be used for their own protection, but the smart money on this side of the Atlantic had it that they needed protection from Champagne Charlie.

The General Court in Massachusetts started the ball rolling by circulating a letter of protest through the other colonies. It was followed within days by a second circular from Virginia.

The Virginia document, calling for a boycott of British goods, was drawn up at a meeting in the Raleigh Tavern in Williamsburg at the urging of George Washington, who said he felt that no one should hesitate to use arms to defend 'liberty which we have derived from our ancestors on which all the good and evil of life depends'.

The document itself was written by a Virginia planter named George Mason. He was not a member of the House of Burgesses, but probably understood Virginia better than any of them. He knew it wouldn't be easy to get his neighbors to join the firebrands from up North. His scheme, then, was to form a voluntary association that required its members to refuse to buy anything British. As an enforcement measure, however, he proposed that members should carefully avoid contact with friends who didn't agree. 'They should be loaded with every mark of infamy and reproach', he suggested. He also suggested that the names of violators should be published in newspapers and that special committees ought to be formed to smoke out people who were secretly buying British imports.

It was probably America's first taste of non-violent protest.

By 1770 all the duties, except a tax on tea, were repealed and the Virginia Grandees were predicting that everybody was going to be happy again. It may have been true in Virginia, but up in Boston the protest was far from non-violent. In December, 1773, a bunch of 'wild Indians' dumped tea valued at £18,000 into Boston harbor. Other colonies followed their example, and thoughtful people were beginning to wonder if America would ever be happy again.

One thing was certain; America was in the mood for a fight.

Thomas Jefferson was among the first to sense the danger. Calling together such men as George Mason and Patrick Henry for another meeting at the Raleigh Tavern, he proposed that communication between the several colonies was critical, and suggested setting up standing 'Committees of Correspondence' to exchange ideas. The Assembly made it official for them, and before long other colonies followed their example. It would become the mortar for uniting them.

After Boston was blockaded by the British in retaliation for their tea party, and Parliament decided to make the Western territories Virginia considered her own part of Quebec, the Virginia Committee called on the others to hold a 'Congress' to figure out what to do next.

It was called the First Continental Congress and was convened at Philadelphia on September 5, 1774. Virginia sent seven delegates, including George Washington and Patrick Henry, and one of the seven, Peyton Randolph, was elected its President.

When the Second Continental Congress met the following spring, George Washington was a delegate again. Adams reported that he '…appeared every day in his military uniform, and by his great experience and abilities in military matters, was of much service to all'. Obviously, the Colonel had future service in mind.

The politics of uniting the colonies was formidable. They all agreed that union was their salvation, but they represented 13 distinct and highly individual entities. They didn't trust each other, and until Thomas Jefferson forced them to set up lines of communication, they had hardly ever even talked to each other.

By 1775, they all knew that war would eventually come, and they knew they would need a leader for a united army. John Hancock of Massachusetts fancied himself the natural choice and others considered themselves just as obvious.

John Adams realized that the Commander-in-Chief could not come from a Northern state if the army was to be truly continental and not just an amalgam of state militias.

As a political consideration, a Southerner would be perfect, and no Southerner was more perfect than George Washington. As a practical consideration, few other men from any colony had the military credentials. Congress elected him Commander-in-Chief on June 14, 1775. An obviously-pleased Adams wrote:

'…The Congress have made choice of the modest, the virtuous, the amiable, generous and brave George Washington Esquire, to be general of the American army, and he is to repair, as soon as possible, to the camp before Boston. This appointment will have a great effect in cementing and securing the union of these colonies. The continent is really in earnest in defending the country.'

Some years later, Adams, a bit less interested in cement, bragged that it was Massachusetts that made Washington a general. All Virginia ever did for him, he snickered, was to make him a colonel.

A few weeks before, a special convention had been held at Richmond to discuss putting Virginia on a footing for war. Patrick Henry fanned the fire with one of the most memorable speeches in the entire pre-revolutionary era. 'He left us all far behind', said Jefferson.

'If we wish to be free', Henry told the convention, 'we must fight!'

He concluded his speech by saying: '…Gentlemen may cry peace, peace …but there is no peace! The war is actually begun. The next gale that sweeps from the north will bring to our ears the clash of resounding arms. Our brethren are already in the field. Why stand we here idle? What is it that gentlemen wish? What would they have? Is life so dear, or peace so sweet, as to be purchased at the price of chains or slavery? Forbid it, Almighty God! I know not what course others may take; but as for me, give me liberty or give me death!'

Then the Virginians put their money where their mouths were. Lord Dunmore, the Royal Governor, had heard about what was going on in Richmond and ordered that the powder from the public magazine should be put aboard British ships in the James River so it wouldn't fall into rebel hands. In response, a company of mountaineers calling themselves 'The Culpeper Minute-Men' marched on the capital to get their powder back. The Governor refused, of course, threatening instead to have the city burned to the ground.

Their leaders, one of whom was John Marshall, who later became Chief Justice of the United States, stood their ground and forced Dunmore to pay heavily for the confiscated powder. After paying the price, he ran for his life and Virginia became the first of the Colonies under direct control of a Colonial Committee of Safety.

The War of Independence might have started right then and there. But up north in Boston, a British general had already beaten them to it.

Two days earlier, General Gage had heard that he would find John Adams and John Hancock in the town of Concord, Massachusetts. He set out from Boston to find them, but only got as far as Lexington, where he met a small army of Minutemen ready for a fight.

It was that army, which grew by 18,000 men within days of the first shot, that General Washington was sent to command.

Washington's seat in the House of Burgesses needed to be filled quickly and the voters of Fairfax County turned to George Mason as the only man capable. Reluctantly, he accepted.

Fearful that the exiled Governor would come back to Williamsburg, the Assembly met in Richmond that summer. Still a reluctant legislator, Mason turned down an offer to serve in the Virginia delegation at the Continental Congress, opting instead to serve on the Committee of Safety which was charged with setting up a whole new Government.

There was great pressure from the people to separate from the British Empire once and for all. Both the Massachusetts and North Carolina delegations at Philadelphia had declared themselves foresquare on the side of independence, but they weren't pushing too hard. War had broken out, to be sure. But Washington had sent General Gage packing toward Canada, and up and down the coast, the mood was wary at best. It's never easy to break away from a mother. Even a mother country.

Finally, Virginia took the bull by the horns. The Virginia Congressional delegation was told to *propose* independence, not just support it. Then the Committee declared Virginia a free and independent Commonwealth and elected Patrick Henry as its governor.

The new Commonwealth had a constitution and a Declaration of Rights. Both were the work of the reluctant delegate, George Mason.

One of the reasons Mason didn't like serving in the Government was that he didn't like political intrigue and hated working in committees. The committee charged with drafting the new plan of government was huge and, in Mason's words, 'overcharged with useless members'.

He worked largely alone, letting the committee members drone on in endless meetings, and eventually produced a document that one of the members admitted 'swallowed up all the rest'.

Mason's words proclaimed that 'all men are by nature equally free and independent and have certain inherent rights'. They declared that 'government is, or ought to be, instituted for the common benefit, protection and security of the people'.

It was a document that would become Virginia's greatest contribution to the new republic. For the first time America said to the world that here in this place man was a naturally free creature, free to do anything at all but threaten or bring harm to anyone.

Mason's constitution for Virginia was the first in America to guarantee a free press. It provided for real religious freedom, too, saying that religion can be 'directed only by reason and conviction, not by force or violence'.

A month after the Virginia constitution was adopted, Richard Henry Lee, who was called 'the American Cicero', was dispatched to Philadelphia to propose to Congress, in the name of Virginia, 'that these united colonies are, and of a right ought to be, free and independent states, that they are absolved from all allegiance to the British Crown, and that all political connection between them and the state of Great Britain is, and ought to be, totally dissolved...'

They were strong words and, though they had been long expected, they brought a gasp from many. In the stunned silence that followed, the delegates decided to postpone voting on the proposal until a proclamation of independence could be written.

They gave that job to one of their youngest members, the 33-year-old Virginian, Thomas Jefferson.

Jefferson was awe-stricken. His choice would have been John Adams of Boston, and he said so. But Adams responded by giving several reasons why Jefferson was better suited:

'Reason first, you are a Virginian and a Virginian ought to appear at the head of this business. Reason second, I am obnoxious, suspected and unpopular. You are very much otherwise. Reason third, you can write ten times better than I can.'

It took Jefferson 17 days to draft the document that began with the words: 'When in the course of human events it becomes necessary for one people to dissolve the political bonds which have connected them with one another...'

It took many days more for Congress to accept the idea. But finally, with John Adams and Benjamin Franklin adroitly fending off the criticism of the fainthearted, the Declaration of Independence was formally adopted, and made official Jefferson's statement that '...We hold these truths to be self-evident that all men are created equal, that they are endowed by their creator with certain unalienable rights, that among these are Life, Liberty and the Pursuit of Happiness'.

It was a tougher statement than George Mason had made, and all the Colonies were committed to it. They also found themselves committed to forming independent governments, and one by one they drafted their own declarations of rights; usually, it was said, with a copy of Mason's Virginia Declaration, a pair of scissors and a jar of paste.

Once having declared independence, the country was bound to go to war to fight for it. Washington had been in New England for a year outfitting and building the Continental Army. But now the British were coming with a vengeance. The day before the new country introduced itself to the world, England's Lord Howe had appeared in the New York area with a considerable army.

The war was generally confined to the Northeast for the next five years. But that's not to say Virginians weren't in the thick of it. One of the men who answered the call was Daniel Morgan, who recruited a band of mountaineers and named them Morgan's Riflemen.

Morgan was tough and so were his men. He walked with a limp because he had once broken a toe kicking a British officer. Most of his teeth were missing after a French bullet had hit him in the side of the neck back in the days of the French and Indian War. After Lexington and Concord his men marched toward Boston to join up with the Continental Army. From there, they pushed on to Quebec. Morgan was so far ahead of them, the British caught him. But the legend says he was so mean they had to let him go. History says that, before they released him, they offered him a commission in their own army.

While they were still in Boston, they met General Washington, who, it was said, got down off his horse and with tears on his face, personally embraced each of the men who had been presented to him as volunteers 'from the right bank of the Potomac'.

Morgan's band turned the tide against the British at Quebec and were the instruments of terror that made the British army surrender at Saratoga. It was that victory that made the French take the war seriously, and by the time the action reached Virginia, one of the commanders of the American army there was a young Frenchman, the Marquis de Lafayette.

The British strategy had been to take the war south and eventually capture Virginia, the richest and most heavily populated of all the Colonies. They began by taking Savannah, then Augusta, in Georgia. Then they moved up to the Carolinas, and in May, 1779, they captured Portsmouth and Suffolk. The war had come home to Virginia.

But the tide was turning against the British in other places, and Virginians were helping to turn it.

One of them was 'Light-Horse Harry Lee' (Henry Lee), who led a force through a thick swamp to overrun a British fort opposite New York City. Another was a young Scottish-born adventurer who had migrated to Virginia and taken a new name to go with his new life. John Paul, who by then called himself John Paul Jones, took the war across the Atlantic. In one of the most dramatic sea battles of any war, he took on a pair of British warships off the East Coast of England. When his own ship, the *Bonhomme Richard*, named in honor of Benjamin Franklin, caught fire and began sinking, the captain of the British ship, *HMS Serapis*, called on him to surrender. 'I have not yet begun to fight!' shouted Jones, and went on to capture the enemy ship before his own went down.

Back in America, the British had captured Charleston and put Lord Cornwallis in charge of leading a leisurely campaign north into Virginia. It wasn't so leisurely.

Most of the British army in the Carolinas was staffed with American Tories. They launched their attack toward Virginia, about a thousand strong, in October, 1780. The Virginians were waiting for them at King's Mountain, just a little south of the Virginia border. The battle was such a rout that William Campbell, the Virginians' leader, was forced to order: 'For God's sake, boys, quit! It's murder to shoot any more!' About 700 were taken prisoner, more than 150 were killed. Many of the prisoners were executed without a trial. One of the Virginian leaders, who ordered the executions, was a man named Charles Lynch, whose name lives on, in infamy, as part of the language.

In December, 1780, a former American officer who had just been commissioned a brigadier general in the British Army arrived at the mouth of the James River with a force of 1,600. Benedict Arnold got as far as Richmond by January 5 and proceeded to set fire to the place. Then he went back down to Portsmouth to set up a winter headquarters. Virginia was in enemy hands.

Virginia was a prize to the British. Arnold would be a prize to the Americans, and to secure the prize, General Washington sent Lafayette south with a force of continental infantry. The French agreed to contribute 1,200 of their own soldiers and a fleet as well. The British Navy intercepted the French ships, and sent 2,600 men to bolster their army. Then they relieved Arnold of his command, snatching the prize from Washington's grasp.

Later in the spring, Lord Cornwallis arrived on the scene looking for a prize of his own. His plan was to capture Lafayette. Cornwallis chased across the state with a force of cavalry, terrorizing everyone in his path, including members of the Legislature, who had been meeting at Charlottesville, and Governor Jefferson, who narrowly escaped an attack on his home and was forced to run for his life into the mountains.

By fall, the British were retreating, and Washington decided to take the offensive. He secretly moved his army down from New York and in mid-September attacked Cornwallis, who had taken refuge at York-town.

The battle went well for the Americans, but Cornwallis had a way to save himself. He thought. He issued orders for his men to cross the York River in barges under cover of darkness, and from there under forced march to retreat to New York. But before they could put the plan into effect, a storm broke out and swamped the barges. And that scuttled the British escape. Hopes of escaping by sea had vanished when the French fleet under the Comte de Grasse took charge of the Chesapeake.

There was nothing left to do but surrender, and the fact that Cornwallis refused to surrender to the Americans, but rather to the commander of the French forces on the scene, didn't stop anybody's joy at all.

A huge dinner was given in Cornwallis' honor attended by top officers of the French, the British and American armies. Among the toasts offered, Cornwallis couldn't resist raising his glass to the health of The King of England, to which Washington quickly added, '...may he stay there!'

The war had ended just a few miles from the place where the ideas that started it all had first been put into words. British bands marching out of Yorktown had been playing a popular tune of the day called 'The World Turned Upside Down'. When Lord North, the English Prime Minister, heard of the surrender, he moaned, 'Oh God! It's all over!'

The world had turned upside down. But for Virginia, 174 years after the first settlers arrived there from England, life was just beginning.

Once the war was over it was time for America to begin acting like a country, but in their squabbles over territory, trade and money, they acted more like children and it looked for a while like the 13 states would never be really united.

Though George Washington thought of him as an almost hopeless provincial, Thomas Jefferson led the way in settling a big argument over territory by giving a huge chunk of Virginia to form five new states. For a lot of reasons, not the least being campaigns fought by Virginians during the war, Virginia claimed all the territory north of the Ohio and east of the Mississippi Rivers. Thanks to Jefferson, it was carved up into Ohio, Indiana, Illinois, Michigan and Wisconsin. Thanks to cooler heads, Jefferson's names for the new states, Assensisipia, Cheronesus and Pelisipia, never made it to any map.

When the time came to draft a constitution for the new country Virginia sent a delegation to Philadelphia that included George Washington, George Mason and Edmund Randolph, as well as James Madison, who many consider did more to put together a workable document than any other delegate.

It wasn't easy. It wasn't easy getting it ratified, either. In Virginia, the debate went on for a month, and ratification carried by a vote of 89 to 79. Up in New York, the Constitution squeaked by with a margin of only three votes.

There was never any question about who would lead

the new republic. Though he said he had no wish '…beyond that of liberty and dying an honest man on my own farm', the 57-year-old George Washington left his farm at Mount Vernon to accept the office of President, a post he would hold for the next 8 years.

He took two Virginians with him to serve in his cabinet, Edmund Randolph as Attorney General and Thomas Jefferson as Secretary of State. Of the first five Presidents, four were Virginians: Washington, Jefferson, Madison and Monroe.

The country's enthusiasm for Washington was almost unanimous. On his trip from Mount Vernon to New York, to accept the Presidency, he was delayed in almost every town by demonstrations of love and affection. In one of the towns he passed under a huge arch that carried the inscription: 'The defender of the mothers will also protect the daughters'. The daughters were presented to him in white robes, singing a hymn that had been composed for the occasion. It included the lines:

'Virgins fair, and matrons grave,
Those thy conquering arms did save,
Build for thee triumphal bowers,
Strew ye fair his way with flowers.'

The man could easily be a king, an emperor, or at the very least, President for life.

He chose instead to retire in 1797, and died two years later. Just two weeks after his funeral, a new century dawned, and along with it a new era, not only for Virginia, but for the whole country.

Even though Virginia had given up the territory to the Northwest, the Old Dominion extended all the way to the Mississippi River when Washington took office. A lot of Virginians had moved west through the Cumberland Gap, along trails Washington himself had explored. But life out there was a good deal different from life on the Tidewater plantations and people who lived there didn't consider themselves Virginians any more. In 1785, they sent a formal petition to Richmond that Fincastle County be given its proper name, Kentucky, and that it ought to be an independent state. Virginia agreed, as long as the frontiersmen agreed to share part of Virginia's war debt. Congress confirmed it in 1792.

In spite of the loss of territory, Virginia grew by leaps and bounds in the early part of the 19th century. Canals were dug to connect the rivers and open the West. People came from all parts of the country to 'take the waters' at places like White Sulphur Springs, Hot Springs and Warm Springs. There wasn't an ailment anyone knew of that Virginia's wonderful water couldn't cure. Railroads were being built, the new Federal city across the Potomac was rising and the Virginian James Monroe was telling the world that European imperialists were no longer welcome on these shores. They called it the Era of Good Feeling. But some people in Virginia weren't feeling so good about what was happening to their State.

The country was growing bigger, stronger and richer. But it was growing faster up north. Virginia seemed to be missing out on the opportunities.

A new aristocracy began to rear its head and it looked to men like Jefferson that their ideals were being forgotten. The new leaders, he said, were trying to 'kindle again the fires'. But if they were missing the boat, most Virginians didn't seem to care.

A thing they all cared about was an issue that sharply divided them: slavery. Men like Jefferson and Madison opposed it violently. James Monroe pushed a scheme that would repatriate blacks to Africa. The Federal Government had passed a law that made importing slaves illegal, but the economy in the South had relied on the institution far too long. The obvious answer was to breed new slaves right here, and that provided a shot in the arm many Virginia planters needed.

What they didn't consider was that they were dealing with people.

One of those people was a giant of a man named Gabriel, who was owned by an Henrico County planter. He and another slave named Jack Bowler conceived a secret plan that called for killing all the whites around Richmond and taking control of the city. After that, it they were successful, they would fan out and take all of Virginia.

Gabriel got word out to nearly all the slaves in the area that he would strike on the night of August 30, 1800, a Saturday. It was customary for blacks to go into town on Saturday nights. This particular Saturday they'd go to Richmond ready to risk their lives for freedom.

The plan was discovered when two slaves told their master what was happening and Governor Monroe was warned in time to call out the militia. Gabriel, meanwhile, had already collected spears and clubs and a small cache of guns. He had visited the state arsenal and taken an inventory of the weapons there and he had a plan for taking them.

His army, which included hundreds of blacks, assembled in a swamp about five miles out of Richmond and decided to attack in spite of the militia. Then a violent thunderstorm washed out bridges and turned roads into seas of mud. Gabriel and his men were stuck in the swamp and Richmond was saved.

Some 50 conspirators were arrested, but Gabriel and Bowler escaped. It was several weeks before they were finally captured at Norfolk and eventually hanged along with 35 others.

Significantly, not all the rebels were hanged. Virginia had a law at the time that required that planters be paid for their property loss if a slave was executed.

A great many blacks in Virginia were free, but the fact was a constant source of tension among poor whites who competed with them for jobs. To compensate for that the state passed a law that any freed slave must leave Virginia within a year of getting his freedom. To satisfy factory owners who hired them in large numbers, the rule was softened to exclude persons who were 'of good character, sober, peaceable, orderly and industrious'. For the others, there was a Catch 22: all the states surrounding Virginia passed laws forbidding free blacks to cross their borders.

To call the situation tense would be a foolish understatement, yet Virginians managed to keep the problem swept under the rug for more than 30 years. Then in 1831, on the day a man in Illinois – by name of Abraham Lincoln – was celebrating his 22nd birthday, there was a solar eclipse in Virginia. It was the signal to a 31-year-old in Southampton County that his time had come.

His name was Nat Turner.

Nat was a deeply religious man who thought strange marks on his head and chest were put there by God as a sign that he was destined to do something special. He had made a break for freedom more than 5 years earlier, but came back to his master because he said God told him to. He also said that God had told him that he should follow in the footsteps of Moses and set his people free.

The February eclipse was the sign he had been waiting for, but he was sick that day and decided to postpone the uprising which he had been planning for years. In the heat of deep summer, the sun changed to a peculiar bluish color, and Nat Turner knew what he had to do.

He slipped into the big house and killed his owner, Joseph Travis, as well as the white man's wife and three children. Then, waving the bloody axe he had used as a murder weapon, he gathered some 60 others and went on a rampage that resulted in the killing of more than 55 whites, many of them women and children. As word of the rebellion spread, panic set in and people from miles around ran for their lives. The militia was called out, even a contingent of U.S. Marines joined the fight. Within 48 hours it was all over, and all of Nat Turner's rebels were either dead or taken prisoner. Turner himself escaped, but was captured two months later and hanged.

Instead of freeing his people, Turner's revolt made life tougher for them. Free blacks were less free, stricter laws in Virginia and all over the South restricted the lives and movements of all blacks. And people who were in favor of slavery became all the more inflexible in their beliefs.

But there was another side to the coin.

There had been an abolitionist movement in America since Colonial times, but in the heart of Dixie no one talked about it much, no matter how right they thought the movement was. In the months following the Turner rebellion, some of those Southerners began coming out of the closet. Among them was Thomas Jefferson's grandson, Thomas Jefferson Randolph and Thomas Marshall, son of the Chief Justice, who said, bluntly, that slavery only 'retards improvement'. On the other hand, men like Thomas R. Dew, a professor at the College of William and Mary, joined other Virginians who dug in their heels to defend the institution. Slavery, he wrote, 'is perhaps the principal means of impelling forward the civilization of mankind'.

Neither side had a prayer of convincing the other of its views; the issue was far too emotional for that. But the fact that both sides had finally gone public had a big effect on the rest of the country. Once more Virginians were putting into words what others were thinking.

Abolitionist thinking had become a fine art in the Northern States, and it seemed to the pro-slavery Virginians that the whole North was ganging up on them. It forced them to retreat even further from the ideals of earlier Virginians who helped to unite the country. They retreated into themselves, and by 1847 had become what President Henry Ruffner of Washington College deplored as:

'...A sparse population, a slovenly cultivation spread out over vast fields that are wearing out, among others that are already worn out and desolate; villages and towns 'few and far between' rarely growing, often decaying, sometimes mere remnants of what they were.'

Yet only a few years before, a visitor from New England had written:

'You would delight in this region, merely to observe the difference in manners and habits, and to experience the princely hospitality of the gentle-born families'.

If the country wasn't following Virginia's lead any longer, neither was the South. The slavery issue had grown to the point where the Southern States had begun talking about seceding from the Union, but when they looked for leadership, they didn't go to Richmond, but to a small city further south, Charleston, South Carolina. No one in Virginia could match the leadership of John C. Calhoun, and the torch was passed to him and other Carolinians.

By the middle of the 19th century, the abolition movement in the North, especially in New England, had reached fever pitch. A Civil War seemed inevitable, and there were plenty of men anxious to provide the spark. One of them was a man named John Brown, who decided that the place to begin the fire had to be Virginia. On the night of October 16, 1859, he led a party of 22 men, including six blacks, across the Potomac at Harpers Ferry. He quickly took the Federal armory there, killed the Mayor and took some of the town's leading citizens into the armory's engine house as hostages.

The Governor asked for Federal help and got it in the form of a company of U. S. Marines, led by Colonel Robert E. Lee, who, like his aide, Lieutenant J. E. B. Stuart, considered himself a Virginian first, an American second.

By the time the Marines arrived, the Virginia Volunteers had already eliminated all of Brown's band, except Brown himself and four others. The fight was quickly brought to an end, Brown was captured, brought to trial and sentenced to hang. Prophetically, Brown said that he was 'worth inconceivably more to hang than for any other purpose'. He was probably right.

News of the hanging spread through the North like a swamp fire. The abolitionists had a martyr and they made the most of it.

When Abraham Lincoln was elected President in 1860, officials in South Carolina had already begun seizing Federal property in their State. The most important prize was Fort Sumter, at the mouth of Charleston harbor, which was in control of the United States Army. On April 12, 1861, Charleston's Palmetto Guards began a cannon assault on the fort. When it fell the following day, the North and the South were at war.

There was no question which side Virginia was on, but the Assembly didn't like the idea of secession. They had their mind made up for them three days later when President Lincoln called on the states to provide volunteers to stop the rebellion. Saying they couldn't 'coerce' a sister state, Virginians answered the call by replacing the Stars and Stripes in front of the State House with the stars and bars of the new Confederate flag.

Late in the spring, Richmond was made capital of the Confederacy and that made it a prime target of the Union Army. The fact that it was the most northerly of the Confederate States, and was just across the river from the United States capital made it obvious that Virginians were going to bear the brunt of the war.

When Virginia seceded, Robert E. Lee, a West Point graduate who was the son of the Revolutionary War hero, 'Light-Horse Harry Lee', resigned his commission in the United States Army, saying he would not draw his sword again '...save in the defense of my native State'. He was immediately made commander-in-chief of Virginia's military, and was later appointed chief military advisor of the Confederacy in a move by its President, Jefferson Davis, to turn the tide of the war, which by then was going badly for the South.

As quickly as the war began, Virginia was forced to give up Accomack and Northampton counties on the Eastern Shore. Then Alexandria fell and stayed in Union hands for the entire war. They captured and held Lee's estate at Arlington, and took control of the Baltimore and Ohio Railroad. In the summer of 1861, more territory slipped away from the Old Dominion when westerners, with less sympathy for the Confederacy, voted to form a new state they would call West Virginia. It didn't become official until 1863, but then 48 Virginia counties seceded from the Confederacy.

Before he got there, the Confederate Army had already attacked McClellan, and Robert E. Lee had been put in charge of defending the city. While most of his men were digging trenches, Lee sent General Jeb Stuart with 1,200 riders to go behind the enemy lines. It was one of the most daring acts of the war. Stuart destroyed essential supplies and brought back important information that allowed Lee to push the Federals back to the James River and save Richmond.

During the summer of 1862, the Rebel Army took the Federal warehouse at Manassas and drove the enemy across Bull Run all the way to Alexandria. Then they took the war to the North by crossing the Potomac into Maryland. They were driven back, but took a stand at Antietam Creek and bought time for an orderly retreat back into Virginia.

The Union Army didn't follow until December, when General Ambrose Burnside attacked Fredericksburg. He lost thousands of men and didn't take the city. The Confederates, on the other hand, managed to pick up shoes and warm clothes from the dead. It was something they needed desperately.

In May, 1863, 'Fighting Joe' Hooker, who had replaced Burnside as the U. S. commander, decided to restart the march on Richmond. He ran into 'Stonewall' Jackson at Chancellorsville. The battle lasted two days, and was far and away the Confederacy's finest hour. But before he sent the enemy packing, Jackson was hit in the arm by a volley fired by his own men who, significantly, were behind him. To save his life, doctors were forced to amputate. The operation prompted Lee

to say, 'He has lost only his left arm. I have lost my right.' Jackson was dead within a few days, but thanks to him, Lee was now ready to take the war North with a vengeance.

By the end of June, 1863, he had pushed up the Shenandoah Valley, through Maryland and into Pennsylvania. His army was scattered, however, and he decided to bring them together at Gettysburg.

When they got there, the Federal Army under General George Meade, had already dug-in on the all-important high ground. The Confederate forces under General James Longstreet fought for two days, but the enemy didn't budge in spite of horrifying losses on both sides.

The heart of Meade's defense was a cannon battery on top of Cemetery Ridge. It had to be taken, but there was a lot of open land in front of it. The job of charging across it and up the hill went to 10,000 men, mostly Virginians, commanded by General George Pickett. They made it to the top, but not before their ammunition was gone and the charge ended in bloody hand-to-hand fighting. Without weapons they couldn't hold the advantage and were forced to retreat. By the time they got back to their own lines only one out of four of the original force was still standing. In the three-day battle, Lee had lost more than 40 per cent of his army. He was forced to retreat back to Virginia where the war would drag on for almost two more years.

The following year, the Union Army began to march on Virginia again, this time with a new commander, General Ulysses S. Grant. His first brush with Lee was in a thick forest west of Chancellorsville where he was defeated. Other Federal generals had always retreated after defeat, but Grant regrouped and pushed on to Spotsylvania Courthouse where the two armies tangled again.

The Confederates once more held their ground, but Grant was determined. He kept moving southeast and by June was within 10 miles of Richmond. Lee's army was between him and his prize and ready to fight. In a battle at Cold Harbor, Grant lost 10,000 of his men in a single hour. In the previous six-week march through Virginia, he lost 55,000, more men than Lee's entire army.

Still Grant kept marching. A month later he began a

siege of Petersburg, which was fiercely defended by a force largely composed of old men and children. While the 10-month siege was going on, General Philip Sheridan swept through the Shenandoah Valley destroying everything in sight.

'When this is completed', he boasted, 'the Valley from Winchester up to Staunton, 92 miles, will have but little in it for man nor beast. A crow cannot fly over it without carrying his own rations.'

It's what passed for wit in the Union Army, but it was no laughing matter in Richmond. Of the 11 Confederate States, eight were effectively out of the war. The Carolinas were blockaded and starting to feel the wrath of Sherman's army. More than half of Virginia was occupied by Federal troops. It was time to think about stopping the war.

President Davis sent peace feelers to President Lincoln, but couldn't agree to Lincoln's terms that the Union must be restored. So the war went on. On April 1, 1865, Petersburg finally fell and two days later, Grant marched on Richmond.

The retreating Confederate troops set fire to warehouses and bridges and in the process destroyed almost all of the downtown section of the city. Union soldiers put out the fires and put an end to the looting that had started. They also raised the Stars and Stripes over the Capitol.

A week later General Lee found himself surrounded. 'There is nothing left for me', he said, 'but to go and see General Grant'.

They met in the home of Wilmer McLean at Appomattox, at noon, on April 9, 1865. 'Our conversation grew so pleasant', reported Grant, 'I almost forgot the object of our meeting'. Even in defeat, the courtliness and dignity of the Virginian was remarkable. Grant offered to disarm the Confederates and let them go free on parole. In his own disarming way, Lee also persuaded him to let them keep their horses and provide them with much-needed rations.

Then came the hard part.

The war between the states had left more destruction in Virginia than in any other place. The old systems that had kept the state in the control of 'well-born' families were wiped out. The mainstay of the economy, slavery, had been eliminated. And then, to add insult to all the injuries, Washington took the name 'Virginia' off the map and renamed it 'Military District Number One'.

But Virginians have always been survivors. In spite of opportunists who streamed down from the North, carpetbags in hand, 'to spread knowledge and culture', they survived. In spite of the patronizing advice of Northerners who told newly-freed blacks, 'you can apply the torch to the dwellings of your enemies', they survived. In spite of the Ku Klux Klan and war veterans who said, 'I won't be reconstructed and I don't give a damn', they survived.

But don't let anyone tell you it was easy.

There were bright spots, too. As a textile center, Danville had grown to four times its original size before 1890. Richmond was rebuilt and growing. People weren't chewing tobacco as much as they did before the war, but a new invention they called cigarettes made tobacco more important than ever and Richmond had plenty to sell. Cities were rebuilt and new ones established, and Virginia slowly moved away from the land into a new and growing urban setting. By the turn of the century, most of the physical scars of the war were gone. The most devasted of all the Southern States was first to rebuild. Virginians have always prided themselves on being first. Their pride carried them through.

Virginia's pride is in its tradition, but the beauty of the place would make anyone proud. Any Virginian will tell you that it's quite the best part of America. From the magnificence of Mount Vernon and Arlington to the excitement of Norfolk and Richmond, to the crystal caves they say can be found under every hill and the quiet beauty of its beaches, not many states offer so much variety. The rich red color of the soil, the soft green of the trees, and the Blue Ridge Mountains offer a landscape that inspires a lot more than simple pride.

T. S. Eliot once said that crossing the Potomac into Virginia was an experience to be compared with crossing the border from Wales to England. Virginia is still much more tied to the Mother Country than any other part of America. In the hills people still talk with the same accents their ancestors brought over from Elizabethan England. In the cities British-cut suits are still the mark of a man. Virginians share the love of their cousins for long walks in the country, a glass of sherry in front of a roaring fire, a good fox hunt, a genteel and traditional way of keeping Christmas.

And the love is often returned. Back before World War I, Winston Churchill enthusiastically reported that a great many Americans, 'including a number of Virginians' had volunteered to fight at England's side.

The Church of England, in the guise of the Protestant Episcopal Church, still dominates in Virginia in spite of the huge Fundamentalist movement that swept the South in the 19th century, and to be a Vestryman is one of the marks of today's gentry.

Some of the best preparatory schools in the country are in Virginia and some of the best of them are run by the Episcopal Church. The best families send their sons to them, then hopefully the lads go on to the University of Virginia. The honor codes are among the strictest in the country, designed to promote conformity, class consciousness, a sense of tradition and, above all, gentility. After the Civil War Robert E. Lee was made president of Washington College. Once, when a new student asked him for a copy of the school's rules, Lee informed him: 'We have but one rule here, and that is that every student must be a gentleman'.

Professional status is important, of course, and there is no better State in the Union for a lawyer to call home. Clergymen rate high as well. But real status comes from how well and how tall you sit in the saddle.

There are more horses in Virginia by far than there are in Texas and, particularly in the northern part of the State, there are hundreds of schools and stables, breeding farms and hunt clubs. Obviously speaking for all Virginians, Robert E. Lee once said of his famous horse, 'Traveller', that he was: 'my only companion, I may say my only pleasure'.

There are 20 formal 'Hunts' in Virginia, including the famous Blue Ridge Hunt which rides to hounds as often as possible during the season, which runs from late October until the middle of March.

Culture rears its head in the heart of Hunt Country at Wolf Trap Farm Park for The Performing Arts. You can hear the sounds of a symphony orchestra there, an opera or a jazz combo under the stars, in a setting that makes it hard to believe that Washington is only 20

minutes away. Sitting there, it's easy to understand why George Washington and his neighbor, George Mason, found Virginia such a wonderful place to live.

George Washington himself said that Mount Vernon was the most 'pleasantly situated' estate in all America. For travelers, at least, he was probably right. It's about 15 miles south of the Washington Monument in the capital. Along with Arlington and Williamsburg, the dozen buildings on the first President's plantation lure more people into Virginia than almost anything else. The smart ones keep going a little further south to Gunston Hall, a fabulous Georgian house that was home to George Mason. As at Mount Vernon, most visitors are impressed by the gardens around it. But even more impressive is the drawing room with all the elegance of an Italian villa and a room full of Chippendale furniture and romantic chinoiserie.

And, of course, getting there is half the fun because between the estates and the District of Columbia you have to pass through Alexandria. With cobblestone streets and fine old 18th-century houses, the city puts you in the mood for any trip into the past.

The past is all around you in Fredericksburg, the place the city fathers humbly call 'America's Most Historic City'. There are occasional cries of protest from Philadelphia and Boston on that claim. But the Virginians have some solid arguments. This is where George Washington spent most of his boyhood. It was where he probably chopped down a cherry tree, and where he skimmed a silver dollar across the Rappahannock. It was where he learned never to tell a lie, and where he became a Freemason. It was where his sister Betty became the wife of planter Fielding Lewis, where his brother Charles operated a tavern and where his mother, Mary Washington, lived in a house he himself had bought for her.

But Washington wasn't the only President associated with Fredericksburg. This is where James Monroe first hung out his shingle as a lawyer and began his rise from the Virginia Legislature to the Continental Congress and eventually to the White House.

John Paul Jones called Fredericksburg home. And this was where the war between the states was probably as its most active because of the location between Richmond and Washington.

Though James Monroe started in Fredericksburg, he flowered in yet another of America's 'most historic' cities, Charlottesville. He had studied law under Thomas Jefferson, and the better he got to know his teacher, the better he liked him. His admiration grew to the point that he packed up his law books and shingle and moved west to be nearer to him. He built a fine house he called Ash Lawn within sight of Jefferson's even finer Monticello.

When he moved in, Mr. Jefferson told him that 'the neighborhood has improved'. It was a neighborhood that already included James Madison. It also included the University of Virginia, which Jefferson had not only founded, but had also designed the buildings, hired the masters and fought for a law that granted it permanent financial support as one of America's first state universities.

His design makes it easily the most beautiful of any of the state universities, and more impressive than most private institutions.

Though a great many people like to be thought of as 'Renaissance men', few can compare with Thomas Jefferson. Architecture was one of his interests and the work of Andrea Palladio one of his passions. Work on the university gave him a chance to follow in the master's footsteps. He began with faculty housing, a series of buildings he called 'pavilions'. Each sported a classical portico which together would give students examples of all the Greek and Roman orders. He had the same complaint many modern builders use as an excuse for bad work. He found there were no skilled carvers and sculptors who could work in the old styles. But unlike today's architects, he found a way to solve the problem. He imported artisans from Italy to do the work. Though Virginia was never a 'melting pot' state, many of the descendants of Jefferson's Italian craftsmen still live in the Charlottesville area.

The houses, connected by arcades, faced each other across a broad lawn which marched in terraces up a gentle hill to the great rotunda, inspired by the Pantheon in Rome. By the time work began on the rotunda, Jefferson had begun importing pediments and capitals from Italy because money was growing too short to import any more people.

To keep money coming, Jefferson the politician made repeated trips to the Legislature with his hat in his hand. When one of his colleagues asked why he didn't make fewer trips and ask for more money at one time, Jefferson the phrase-maker said it was because, 'no one likes to have more than one hot potato crammed down his throat at any one time'.

The university was his proudest accomplishment. But his great monument is the home he designed for himself and called Monticello, 'little mountain'. The house is as fine as any villa Palladio built on the Venetian Plain and the inventive 'modern improvements' Jefferson incorporated into his design would have made the master proud.

American planters had always built big, impressive houses, but kept the stables and smokehouses, schoolhouses and dairies, even the kitchens, housed in outbuildings. Jefferson followed the Italian style of connecting the buildings and concealing them behind and under terraces.

In the center, the 35-room house is dominated by an octagonal dome. Inside are mementoes of the man, including furniture he designed for the house, a dumbwaiter he built to save trips to the wine cellar and a clock that only has to be wound once a week.

Jefferson died on July 4, 1826, 50 years to the day after his Declaration of Independence was first read. The inscription he wrote for his tombstone doesn't mention that he had been a Governor of Virginia, Minister to France, Secretary of State or even President of the United States. The inscription identifies him as 'Author of the Declaration of Independence; of the Statute of Virginia for Religious Freedom; and the Father of The University of Virginia'.

He loved Virginia, and the place he chose to live is in an area they call the 'Piedmont', from the Latin for 'foothills'. To the west of it, the beautiful Blue Ridge Mountains rise gently from the plain. To the east, the Tidewater area is totally different, with sandy soil and rolling plains. Richmond, Petersburg and other major cities mark its western boundary at a point called the 'Fall Line', where the rivers are marked with falls and rapids. It was the furthest west Colonial ships would navigate, and though the line marked the edge of civilization for generations, cheap water power made it a thriving edge.

In the early days, the Piedmont was a garden spot.

Once settlers began moving in, they found the soil free from stones and easy to cultivate. Spring came early to the hills and fall came late. To men like Jefferson, it was a Garden of Eden.

Beyond the Blue Ridge, the Virginia Valley extends more than 350 miles from the Shenandoah in the North to the 'mountain empire' in the Southwest. The Shenandoah flows in a northerly direction and Valley natives, traveling toward Winchester from the South, will say they're going 'down the Valley'. It's confusing, but they're right.

The rock formation called Natural Bridge, once owned by Jefferson, is Virginia's best-known natural attraction. But Virginians say Balcony Falls, on the James River, is the State's most beautiful spot. It's easy to compare for yourself. They're only a couple of miles apart.

Across the Chesapeake in the East, Virginia becomes something quite different in the place they call the Eastern Shore. The first settlers didn't even call it Virginia, preferring to keep to the original Indian name, 'Accawmacke', meaning 'land beyond the waters'. The London Company went along with it, addressing its multitude of orders and communications to 'Ye Colonie of Virginia and the Kingdom of Accawmacke'.

People who still live in the Kingdom live largely off the sea and their catches of crabs and oysters make some of the best eating in America. It's a simple life, but rewarding, and it shows in the people who are quick to tell you that wild horses couldn't drag them off their beautiful peninsula.

And there are plenty of wild horses there to do the job. They say a Spanish galleon ran aground on Assateague Island back in the 16th century, dumping a cargo of horses bound for Mexico. Their descendants are still there, running wild on what is now a National Seashore.

Once a year, at the end of July, the horses are rounded up and herded across the channel from Assateague to the smaller Chincoteague Island where they are put up for auction. The event is a week-long festival with fairs and special entertainment and, of course, Virginia's favorite attraction, lots of horses. When it's all over, the unsold horses swim back across the channel to the big island. The event lures thousands to the shore, it helps keep the herd thinned out and it provides good Virginia homes for some very good horses.

The seashore extends to the mainland and to one of the most famous beaches on the Eastern seaboard, Virginia Beach. The season begins early there with the annual saltwater fishing tournament in June. Then, a month later, culture raises its head high with a boardwalk art show that attracts hundreds of artists from all parts of the country, not to mention thousands of art lovers and buyers. It's one of the best places for surfing on the East Coast, too, and when beaches further north are beginning to close down for the season, Virginia Beach marks the middle of its season by hosting the East Coast Surfing Championships.

You can swim in the ocean right through October at Virginia Beach. But people who love Virginia best head for the hills around that time of year. A lot of them start early enough to catch the Old Fiddlers Contest down in Galax. Then they mosey on down toward the Cumberland Gap hunting for antiques, listening to bluegrass music in the places where bluegrass was born. It's a quiet place, except for the pickin' and strummin', with endless pine forests and long vistas that make you wonder why Daniel Boone was so anxious to head west.

Virginians usually head north when they reach the Gap. It's the way to get to the most beautiful highway anywhere in America, the 105-mile Skyline Drive.

The Drive runs through Shenandoah National Park and over the Blue Ridge Mountains. The Park covers some 300 square miles of virgin forest with plenty of winding paths for hikers and trails for exploring on horseback. Its trout streams are among the best this side of Scotland. And under the mountains, which rise as high as 4,000 feet, there's a whole other world to explore in eight major caverns, including the world-famous caverns of Luray. The underground world is quiet, beautiful, colorful. There are rivers, lakes and waterfalls in a glistening setting that hasn't changed in centuries. And awesome rock formations that have been stirring human imaginations for hundreds of years.

Outdoor rock formations, in the area called Natural Chimneys, form a backdrop for a trip back nearly 200 years, when the descendants of the Virginia Cavaliers descend on Mount Solon for the annual jousting tournament. After having selected a 'Queen of Love and Beauty', the horsemen compete for her attention in the same way their medieval ancestors did: the hard way.

Ask a Virginian when's the best time to visit the Shenandoah and you'll get a lot more than one answer. In the spring it's a wonderland of dogwood and azalea, with rhododendron and daffodils competing for attention. In the summer, wildflowers take over. And in the fall the colors explode at the edges of rolling farmland and spread like fire over the hills. In winter snow usually softens the landscape, and skiers arrive in full force to take advantage of it. But if no one can agree on when's the best time to see it, most will tell you it's a wonderful place to lose yourself. And come out the other side better for the experience.

The Virginia experience is as varied as any to be found in whole groups of other states. Its mountains and valleys, seashores and thriving metropolitan centers. Its historic houses, memorials and battlefields. Its spectacular 'theme-parks' like King's Dominion, where you can take a safari by monorail; or Jamestown Festival Park with restorations of the ships that brought the first English settlers to Virginia; or Busch Gardens, where you can get an idea where they came from.

The Old Country at Williamsburg's Busch Gardens is almost as big an attraction as the restored city itself. It's a trip to England, with a restoration of Shakespeare's Globe Theater, redone American-fashion, three times its original size. It's a peek at Scotland, with bagpipe music in the air and a screaming ride on the spectacular rollercoaster they call the Loch Ness Monster.

There's a smaller rollercoaster in the section that claims to recreate old Germany, and oompah music served with Knackwurst and Sauerkraut. And just across the way, a European-style circus performs in an area with a distinct French flavor.

The park's promoters say it's a way to catch the charm of Europe for a fraction of the cost. They may be right, but it's also in the heart of the area most people go to capture the charm of Virginia.

Previous page: **Dulles International Airport silhouetted by the pale golden light of the setting sun.**

These pages: **Arlington National Cemetery occupies some 500 acres on the sloping, peaceful shores of the Potomac River. Arlington County was a part of the District of Columbia, but originally formed an integral region of Virginia to which it has now returned. This land was once owned by Robert E. Lee. Buried here are William Howard Taft and General John Pershing.**

This page: far right **the gravestone of President Kennedy.** Above and right **the memorial stones of countless soldiers who have fallen in combat for this country.** Above right and opposite page: **the Memorial Amphitheater which is used for Memorial and Veteran Day services.**

This page: above spectators watch the guard of honor marching past the Tomb of the Unknowns. This memorial commemorates the unknown fallen warriors from two World Wars and the Korean War. *Top right* a member of the Old Guard, the oldest active infantry unit of the U. S. Army, changes guard every hour. *Top center* the simple grave of Senator Robert Kennedy. *Right* rows of white tombstones cover the hillside in Arlington Cemetery, with the Washington Monument in the background. *Far right and opposite page:* when the U. S. Marines fought their way to the top of Mount Suribachi on Iwo Jima, in 1945, photographer Joe Rosenthal was there to record the historic moment when Old Glory was raised. The statue, by Felix De Waldron, was based on the photograph and is the U. S. Marine Corps War Memorial.

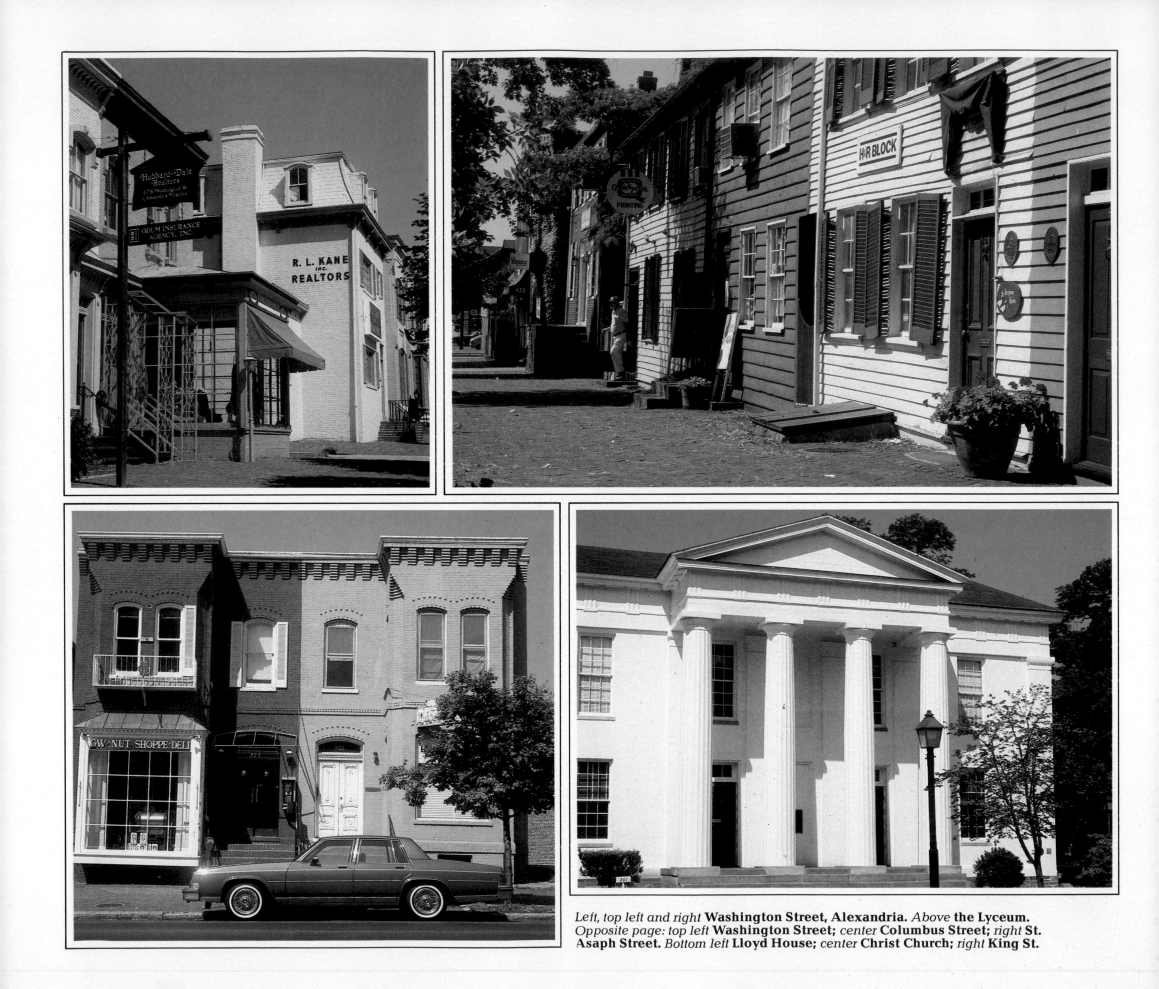

Left, top left and right **Washington Street, Alexandria.** *Above* **the Lyceum.**
Opposite page: top left **Washington Street;** *center* **Columbus Street;** *right* **St.
Asaph Street.** *Bottom left* **Lloyd House;** *center* **Christ Church;** *right* **King St.**

These pages: **just across the Potomac River from Washington, D. C., is Alexandria. One of its attractions is the George Washington Masonic National Memorial. Within this building can be seen the marbled magnificence of the Great Hall.**

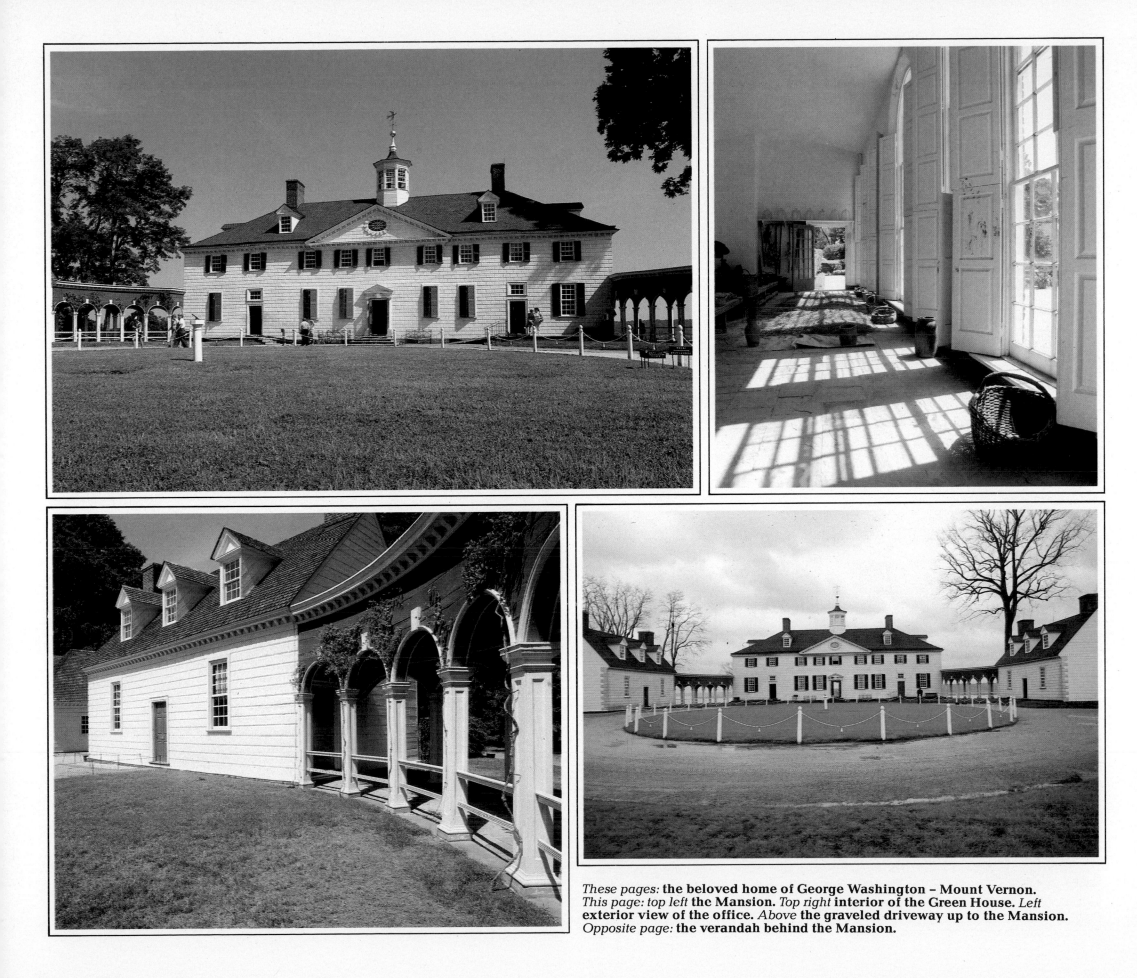

These pages: **the beloved home of George Washington – Mount Vernon.**
This page: top left **the Mansion.** *Top right* **interior of the Green House.** *Left*
exterior view of the office. *Above* **the graveled driveway up to the Mansion.**
Opposite page: **the verandah behind the Mansion.**

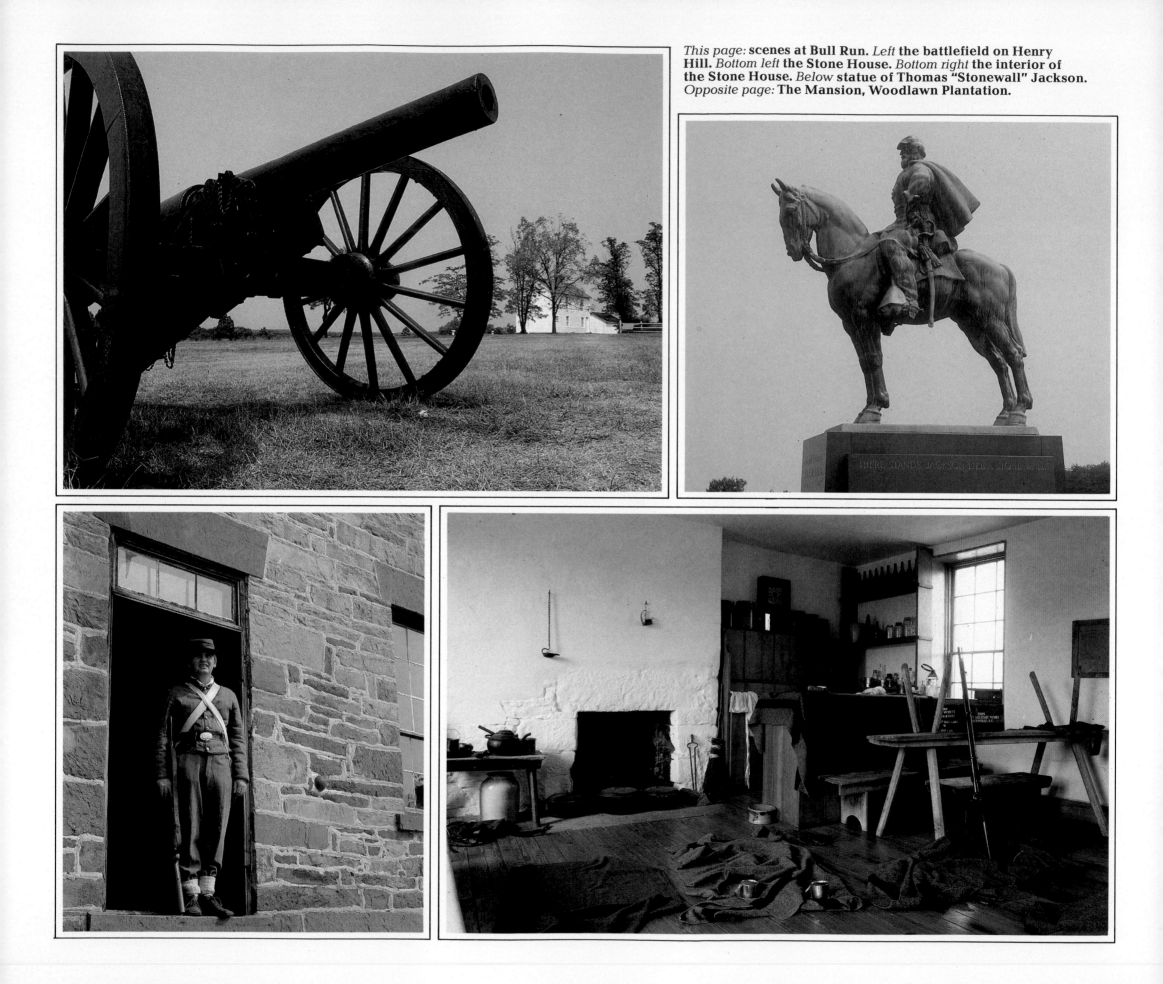

This page: **scenes at Bull Run.** *Left* **the battlefield on Henry Hill.** *Bottom left* **the Stone House.** *Bottom right* **the interior of the Stone House.** *Below* **statue of Thomas "Stonewall" Jackson.** *Opposite page:* **The Mansion, Woodlawn Plantation.**

This page: **sunset silhouettes a tree, its limbs and branches traced upon the clouds of evening, at Cumberland Gap in the Berland Mountain Range.**
Opposite page: **the Great Falls boil into white water upon the rocks of Great Falls River.**

This page: the new timbers of this covered bridge in the Shenandoah Valley stand out in stark contrast against the winter snow.
Opposite page: a farm nestles in the shelter of a tree-fringed valley near Rose Hill.

These pages: **the famous and fast-flowing Shenandoah River at Harpers Ferry, in the Blue Ridge Mountains. This is where West Virginia, Virginia and Maryland all converge. It was selected as the site for the Federal Armory by George Washington.**

This page: the scene at Harpers Ferry, which is
situated at the confluence of the peaceful Potomac and
the tumbling waters of the Shenandoah River.
Opposite page: the old Harpers Ferry footbridge
pictured in the fall.

These pages: **the railroad bridge at Harpers Ferry. It was here, in October 1859, that John Brown launched his anti-slavery raid against the County Militia and Citizen Volunteers in a bid to capture the arsenal and**

In April 1861, a strong force of Virginia militia
marched on Harpers Ferry *these pages*. The Confederates
held the town for two months. *This page:* the fire house
of the old U. S. Armory where John Brown, the
abolitionist, was barricaded in October 1859.

Right **near Luray is the Shenandoah National Park Headquarters. A short journey across the Shenandoah Valley will bring you to the state of West Virginia, once part of the "Old Dominion".** *Top left* **a day trip might include a visit to Harpers Ferry, where John Brown led his unsuccessful rebellion of slaves.** *Above* **a Shenandoah farm at Harpers Ferry.** *Top right* **the dry goods store.** *Opposite page:* **inside the dry goods store at Harpers Ferry.**

These pages: **New Market Battlefield Park. In 1864, the
Confederate general, Breckenridge, ordered the cadets
from the Military Institute into active service. After
marching 90 miles in 3 days they were sent to the front
line by mistake, fighting heroically to win the battle.**

Opposite page: **along the Blue Ridge Parkway Mabry Mill stands, seemingly untouched by the passage of time, as a monument to the days when water was power.**
This page: **cattle graze the meadows of Dan Farm on the Blue Ridge Parkway.**

These pages: the rich colors of fall bring fresh
splendor to the beauty contained within these scenes of
farms nestled among the Ground Hog Mountain landscape
of the Blue Ridge Parkway. The golden reds of nature's
bounty are set among a myriad shades of green.

This page: top left on the Chatham Estate a 'Union soldier' tends his campfire. *Top center* as part of the Fredericksburg and Spotsylvania National Military Park can be seen the regimental monument at Bloody Angle. *Above* on Marye's Heights is the Hugh Mercer Monument. *Far left* the statue and monument of Brigadier General Andrew Atkinson Humphries. *Left* the Thomas Jefferson Freedom Monument.

Opposite page: top left a painting depicting the opening scene of the Battle for Fredericksburg. *Top right* the Richard Kirkland Monument. *Far right* one of the cannons of the Washington Artillery. *Right* a plaque commemorating the Fredericksburg Campaign.

FREDERICKSBURG CAMPAIGN

December 13, 1862. On this ridge, called Marye's Heights, blazed the cannon of Col. J. B. Walton's Louisiana battalion, the Washington Artillery. Late in the day, out of ammunition, it yielded the post to Col. E. P. Alexander's Reserve Artillery. Gen. Robert Ransom's North Carolina infantrymen supported the guns and reinforced Cobb's Georgians and Kershaw's South Carolinians in the Sunken Road below. The open field of attack was raked "as with a fine-tooth comb," Alexander assured corps commander James Longstreet. "A chicken could not live on that field."

United States Department of the Interior   National Park Service

IN MEMORIAM
RICHARD ROWLAND KIRKLAND
CO. G, 2ND SOUTH CAROLINA VOLUNTEERS
C. S. A.

AT THE RISK OF HIS LIFE, THIS AMERICAN
SOLDIER OF SUBLIME COMPASSION BROUGHT
WATER TO HIS WOUNDED FOES AT
FREDERICKSBURG. THE FIGHTING MEN ON
BOTH SIDES OF THE LINE CALLED HIM
"THE ANGEL OF MARYE'S HEIGHTS."

FELIX DE WELDO
SC. 1965

This page: along Caroline Street, in Fredericksburg, can be seen many fine examples of colonial architecture among the houses, shops and restaurants. An early fort was established in this area in 1676 and by 1727 the city of Fredericksburg was founded. On April 29, 1775, it declared its independence from England. The region suffered enormously during the Civil War as the tide of battle swept the land. Four major engagements took place near the city: Chancellorsville, the Wilderness, Spotsylvania and Fredericksburg.

Opposite page: at 1201 Washington Avenue is Kenmore; the home of George Washington's only sister, Betty Washington Lewis, and her husband, Colonel Fielding Lewis. The building dates from some time after 1752, and retains much of its original woodwork, paneling and plasterwork. It is tastefully furnished with 18th-century antiques.

THE CHIMNEYS
Publick House
CIRCA 1769

LUNCH
MON.-SUN. 11:30-3:00
DINNER
TUES-WED-THURS-SUN 5:30-9:30
FRI-SAT 5:30-10:00 CLOSED MON EVES

This page: **the George Washington Birthplace Monument.** *Below* **the kitchen area.** *Right* **the farm buildings.** *Bottom left* **plaque at the burial ground.** *Bottom right* **inside the weaving room.** *Opposite page:* **farm buildings and workshops.**

In Memory of the American Kindred and Children of the Ancestors of George Washington. Their remains repose here beneath but their names as once here inscribed, have been effaced by the relentless hand of Time.

This page: **inside the Hugh Mercer Apothecary Shop, with its gleaming glass exhibits. Dr. Mercer was a close friend of George Washington who came to him for advice on many occasions.** *Opposite page:* **this splendid interior demonstrates Virginian style and elegance.**

These pages: **concentrated within Virginia is some of the finest domestic architecture in the country, most of it on the Tidewater peninsulas of the old river plantations. Combined with Colonial Williamsburg, the heritage of Virginia is seen as a rich-woven tapestry.**

These pages: **the Old South still lives on in Virginia. Wherever you visit in the state there are reminders of the days of the Old Dominion, its traditions and values. The remaining plantation house mansions serve as fine examples of the proud heritage of Virginia.**

These pages: **the Rising Sun Tavern in Fredericksburg was built about 1760 by George Washington's youngest brother, Charles. Colonial leaders on the way to the Continental Congress in Philadelphia would stop here.** *This page:* **the tap room.** *Opposite page:* **the Great Room.**

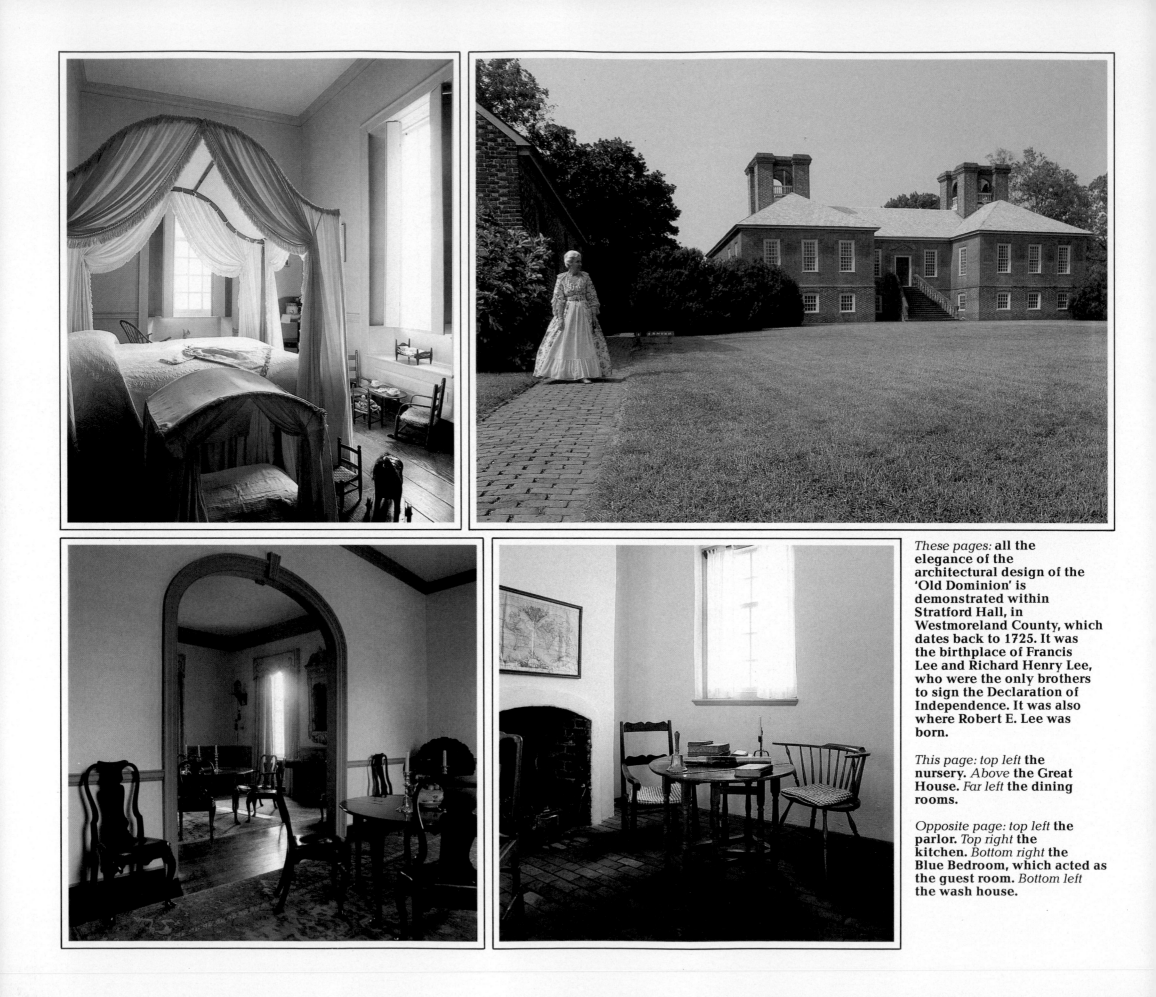

These pages: all the elegance of the architectural design of the 'Old Dominion' is demonstrated within Stratford Hall, in Westmoreland County, which dates back to 1725. It was the birthplace of Francis Lee and Richard Henry Lee, who were the only brothers to sign the Declaration of Independence. It was also where Robert E. Lee was born.

This page: top left the nursery. Above the Great House. Far left the dining rooms.

Opposite page: top left the parlor. Top right the kitchen. Bottom right the Blue Bedroom, which acted as the guest room. Bottom left the wash house.

This page: **Popes Creek Plantation, reconstructed to show the environment of George Washington's birthplace.**
Opposite page: **started in 1769, Monticello was the beautiful home of Thomas Jefferson and is regarded as a classic example of American architecture.**

Left the statue of Thomas Jefferson outside the University Rotunda Building. *Top left* a statue of Homer and his young guide in front of Cabell Hall. *Top right* the Medical School, University of Virginia, Charlottesville. *Above* Monticello House. *Opposite page:* on the campus of the University.

This page: the Meadow Run gristmill and general store, near Charlottesville, dates from 1797. *Opposite page:* the Mitchie Tavern Museum. Built in 1735, Patrick Henry lived here as a child. John Mitchie bought it in 1746 and made it into a tavern.

This page: top left the statue of Thomas Jonathan Jackson in Old Charlottesville. *Top center* statue in memory of James Rogers McConnell which is inscribed, "Soaring like an Eagle, into new Heavens of Valor and Devotion". He was killed in battle while serving with the Volunteer Army of France on March 19, 1917. *Left* in Lee Park the statue of Robert E. Lee. *Above* the James Monroe Statue. *Opposite page:* a reconstructed logging railroad on the Blue Ridge Driveway.

JAMES MONROE
1758–1831

Opposite page: **Lake Sharando is a well-known and popular swimming and recreation center.** *This page: right* **a turkshead lily along the shores of Lake Sharando.** *Top right* **the Saltpeter Cave at Natural Bridge, which was worked during the Civil War and was vital for the production of gunpowder.** *Above* **a water cascade on the Blue Ridge Driveway.**

In north central Virginia, at Staunton near West Virginia, the 28th President of the United States was born. Thomas Woodrow Wilson's birthplace was at the "Manse" of the First Presbyterian Church on December 28, 1856. A professor of jurisprudence and allied subjects at several universities, he decided to enter politics as a Democrat. In 1912 he became governor of New Jersey and President in 1913. He led the U. S. into World War I in 1917 and proposed the Fourteen Points in 1918 as a basis of peace. He secured the formation of the League of Nations, but the U. S. Senate refused to give it support. He was given the Nobel peace prize in 1919 and retired from office in 1921. *This page: top left* the workroom kitchen. *Left* a bedroom. *Above* Woodrow Wilson's old university desk. *Opposite page:* the parlor.

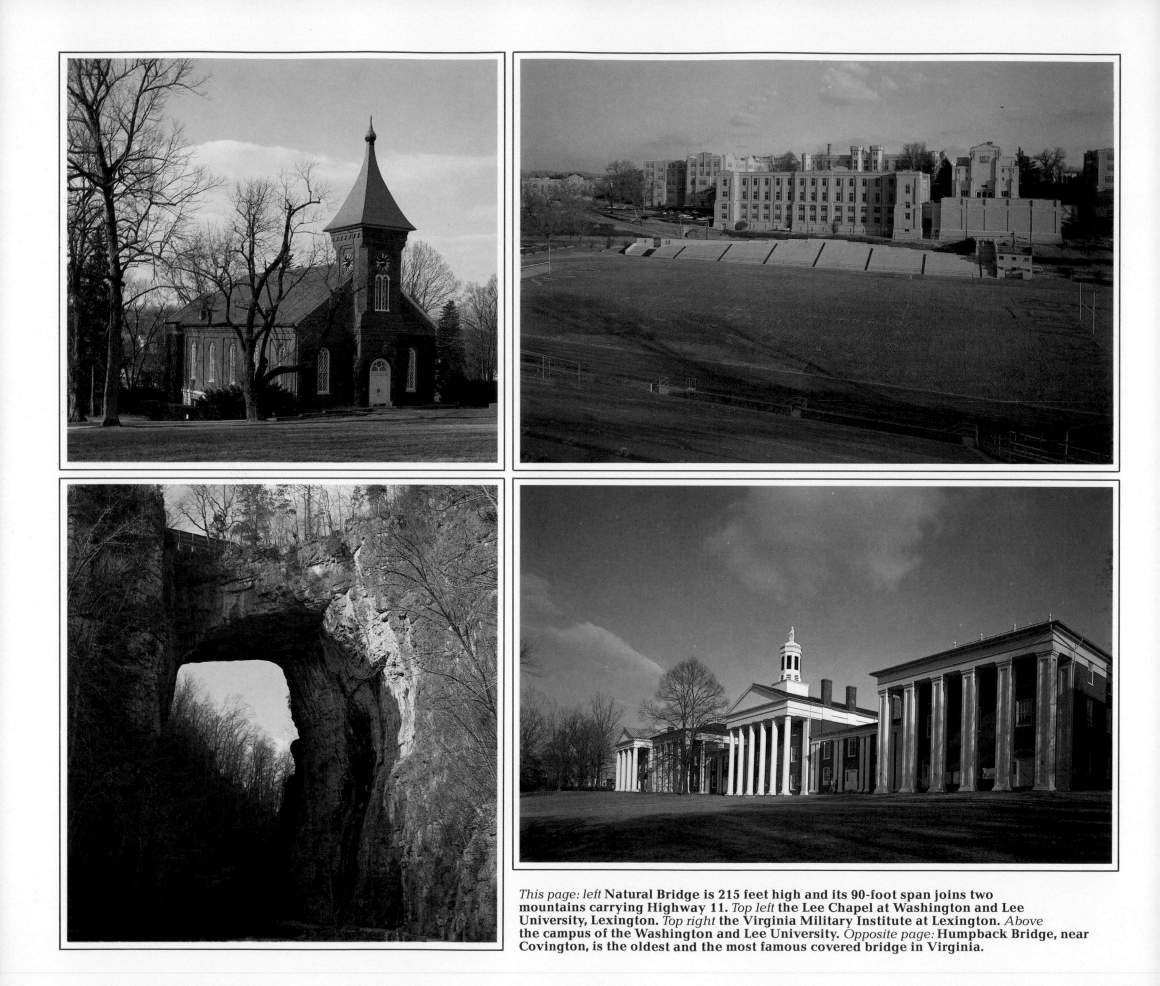

This page: left **Natural Bridge is 215 feet high and its 90-foot span joins two mountains carrying Highway 11.** *Top left* **the Lee Chapel at Washington and Lee University, Lexington.** *Top right* **the Virginia Military Institute at Lexington.** *Above* **the campus of the Washington and Lee University.** *Opposite page:* **Humpback Bridge, near Covington, is the oldest and the most famous covered bridge in Virginia.**

These pages: the city of Roanoke is situated 175 miles southwest of Richmond, on the Roanoke River. It was charted in 1874 as the town of Big Lick, but was renamed Roanoke after the Indian term for "shell money". Manufactured products include railway cars, clothing, chemicals, furniture, and steel and metal goods. *Top left and bottom left* the Hollins College for Women was founded in 1842. In 1966, the Virginia Western Community College was formed. *Above* Hotel Roanoke. *Left* St. Andrew's Church and bell tower. *Opposite page:* the city seen sprawled across Roanoke Valley. It houses the headquarters of the Jefferson National Forest and within its corporate limits is 610-metre Mill Mountain. Southeast of the city is the childhood home of Booker T. Washington, the educator.

This page: **cattle grazing at Appomattox Court House National Historical Park.** *Opposite page:* **the tobacco house at the Booker T. Washington National Monument. This man was born a slave, but later founded Tuskegee Institute, Alabama, a top center for Negro education.**

These pages: **on April 9, 1865, General Robert E. Lee surrendered the army of Northern Virginia to General Ulysses S. Grant at the Appomattox Court House. The site now forms the centerpiece of a National Historical Park.** *Top left* **the guest house.** *Top right* **Isabell House.** *Left* **the Kelly House.** *Above* **Meeks store.** *Opposite page:* **a plaque within the National Park.**

FROM THIS SPOT WAS FIRED
LAST SHOT FROM THE ARTILLARY
OF THE ARMY OF NOTHERN VIRGINIA,
ON THE MORNING OF APRIL 9TH,
1865.

These pages: **various faces of Richmond.**
Top left and top right **downtown skyline.**
Bottom left **reflection of City Hall in the**
Richmond Ear and Eye Hospital. *Above*
Shockoe Slip. *Center* **St. Mark's Episcopal**
Church. *Opposite page:* **the James River.**

This page: **the mansion house on the Shirley Plantation which was built from 1720-40. The estate has been owned by the Carter family since the 17th century.** *Opposite page:* **the mansion of the Westover Plantation was built in 1730-34 by William Byrd II, founder of Richmond.**

This page: the Berkeley Plantation is where the first
official Thanksgiving service in America was held, on
December 4, 1619. It was also the headquarters of Gen.
McClellan in the Seven Days' Battles of the Civil War.
Opposite page: Sherwood Forest Plantation's mansion.

Charles City lies east of Richmond along Virginia 5. It is known for its magnificent plantations which lie near the James River. *These pages:* **John Tyler, the 10th President, bought Sherwood Forest in 1842, and lived there for the remaining 20 years of his life.**

These pages: **the Petersburg National Battlefield was the scene of ten months of war between the Union armies of the James and the Potomac, and that of the Confederates under General Robert E. Lee and P. G. T. Beauregard. The right of the Confederate forces was eventually crushed at Five Forks, which led to the evacuation of Petersburg. The siege lasted from June 15, 1864, to April 2, 1865. Total troop losses amounted to some 70,000 men.**

This page: top left **Union soldier at the company desk of Battery No. 9.** *Above* **a Confederate cannon.** *Far left* **Loading and firing the gun.** *Left* **inside the Sutler Store.**

Opposite page: top left **cannon at Fort Morton.** *Top right and bottom right* **loading and firing the Confederate cannon.** *Bottom left* **gun detachment with the battle flag of the Washington Artillery.**

These pages: the city of Williamsburg has the largest group of restored and reconstructed 18th-century buildings in the world. The effect of visiting the area is like stepping back in time to a bygone age, when horses were the means of transport and the tallest building in town was the church steeple.

These pages: scenes from Colonial Williamsburg.

This page: a soldier stands holding a musket, nicknamed the Brown Bess. *Left and bottom center* black musicians and storytellers. The Company of Colonial Performers revive music of Africa and 18th-century Afro-American music. *Bottom left* the carpenters' yard and woodshed. *Bottom right* a basket weaver.

Opposite page: top left chuck wagon with the guard house behind. *Top right* horse-drawn carriage. *Bottom left* Colonial Street. *Bottom right* Duke of Gloucester Street.

The initial settlement in the area of Williamsburg was in 1633 when the Jamestown settlers raised a palisade across the peninsula to help protect themselves against Indian raids. Restoration of the district began in 1927.

These pages: **Colonial Williamsburg contains many picturesque buildings, including** *left* **a working windmill. The preservation project owes everything to the efforts of Reverend W. A. R. Goodwin and John D. Rockefeller Jr. It is administered by the Colonial Williamsburg Foundation, which also provides cultural and educational programs.**

This page: top left **the Governor's Palace, facing the Palace Green, is the most elegant of the buildings in Williamsburg, and is surrounded by 10 acres of beautiful gardens. The original palace was completed back in 1720, but tragedy struck in 1781 when it was destroyed by fire. The first two state governors, Patrick Henry and Thomas Jefferson, lived here, as did seven royal governors in the days when Virginia was ruled by the British Crown.**

Opposite page: **scene in Colonial Williamsburg.** *This page: left* **the general court room in the Capitol.** *Bottom right* **the council chamber. The Capitol is a reconstruction of the original 1705 building which was destroyed by fire in 1747.** *Below* **the Governor's Palace kitchen.** *Bottom left* **the Raleigh Tavern was the local political and social center; Washington, Jefferson and Henry all met there.**

These pages: **Williamsburg was the capital of Virginia between 1699 and 1799, and retains its colonial atmosphere to this day. The Colonial Williamsburg Foundation helps the town to preserve this important part of America's heritage.**

This page: **Orlando Jones House on Duke of Gloucester Street, Colonial Williamsburg. Besides reconstruction, eighty-eight buildings have survived in this district from the 18th and early 19th centuries.** *Opposite page:* **the Loch Ness Monster roller coaster in Busch Gardens.**

This page: the cool, shaded verdancy of tranquil
**Colonial Williamsburg. The total effect of this area is
one of relaxation and peace, a sense of one's link with
the past, the glory that is America.**
Opposite page: **the mighty waters of the Potomac River.**

These pages: **six miles southeast of Colonial Williamsburg is the Georgian mansion of Carter's Grove, built in 1750-53. In the early 1700s, Robert "King" Carter, the richest of the Virginia planters, bought the 1,400 acres of land upon which his grandson, Carter Burwell, built the three-story mansion house. Fine workmanship in loblolly-pine and walnut helps make this, arguably, the most beautiful house in America.**

These pages: **Jamestown Festival Park is situated a short distance from the original settlement.** *Left* **ruins from the first buildings erected in 1607.** *Bottom right* **the statue of John Smith, governor of Virginia, without whose leadership the colony may well have foundered.**

This page: top left a full-size replica of the *Susan Constant*, which lies in Jamestown Festival Park. The original ship, along with *Godspeed* and *Discovery*, had set sail from England on December 20, 1606. *Above* goats inside the encampment of James Fort. *Left* inside the apothecary building of the fort. *Far left* the statue of Pocahontas, the Indian princess and daughter of the Indian Chief Powhatan, by William Ordway Partridge. Her marriage to John Rolfe brought peace to the settlers, which lasted until five years after her death. Then, in 1622, during the ensuing fighting, perhaps a quarter of the settlers were killed. It was with the introduction of tobacco as a cash crop for export, the achievement of John Rolfe, that the colony began to prosper.

Opposite page: the ruins of a house and tavern demonstrate the relentless effect of passing time.

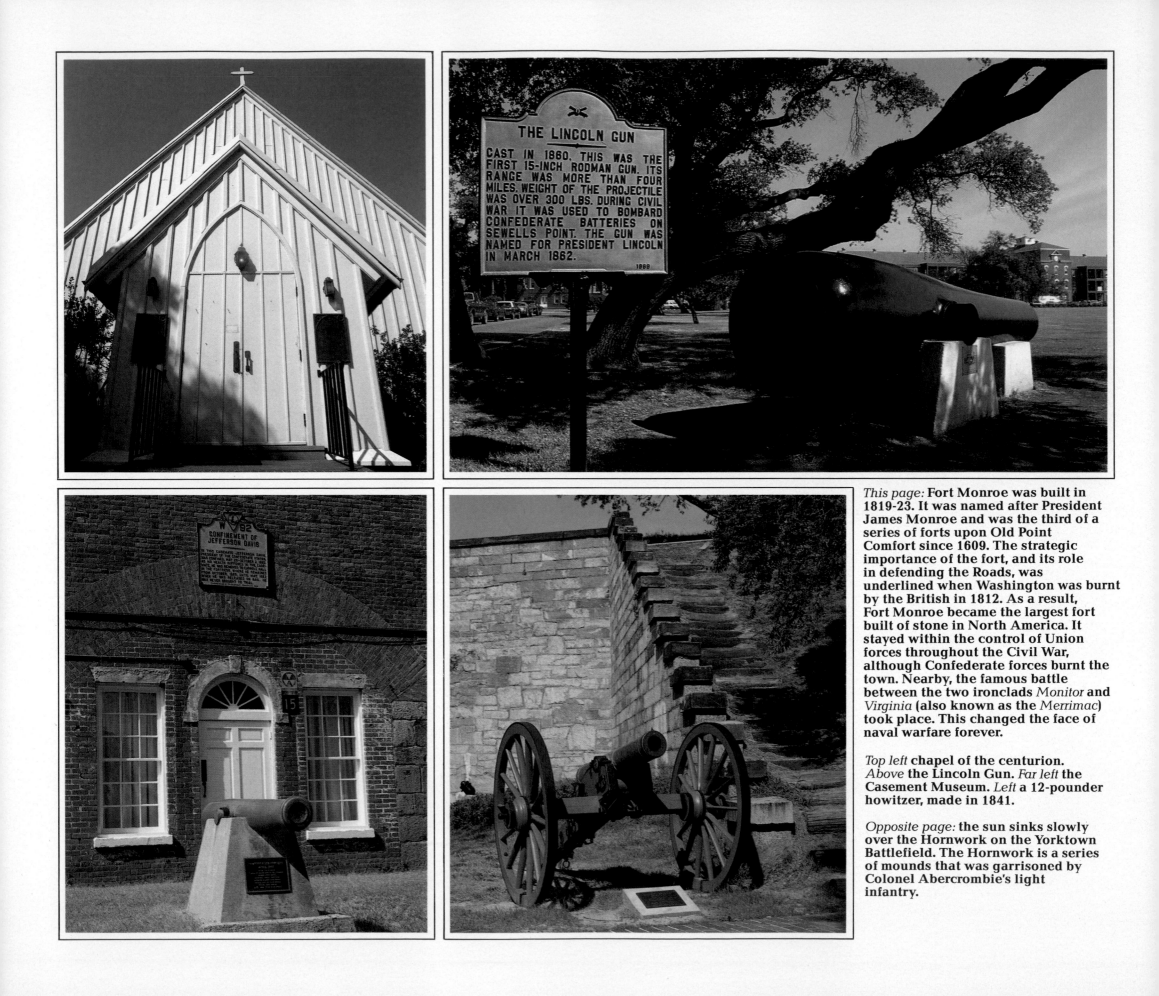

THE LINCOLN GUN

CAST IN 1860, THIS WAS THE FIRST 15-INCH RODMAN GUN. ITS RANGE WAS MORE THAN FOUR MILES. WEIGHT OF THE PROJECTILE WAS OVER 300 LBS. DURING CIVIL WAR IT WAS USED TO BOMBARD CONFEDERATE BATTERIES ON SEWELLS POINT. THE GUN WAS NAMED FOR PRESIDENT LINCOLN IN MARCH 1862.

1969

This page: **Fort Monroe was built in 1819-23. It was named after President James Monroe and was the third of a series of forts upon Old Point Comfort since 1609. The strategic importance of the fort, and its role in defending the Roads, was underlined when Washington was burnt by the British in 1812. As a result, Fort Monroe became the largest fort built of stone in North America. It stayed within the control of Union forces throughout the Civil War, although Confederate forces burnt the town. Nearby, the famous battle between the two ironclads** *Monitor* **and** *Virginia* **(also known as the** *Merrimac***) took place. This changed the face of naval warfare forever.**

Top left **chapel of the centurion.** *Above* **the Lincoln Gun.** *Far left* **the Casement Museum.** *Left* **a 12-pounder howitzer, made in 1841.**

Opposite page: **the sun sinks slowly over the Hornwork on the Yorktown Battlefield. The Hornwork is a series of mounds that was garrisoned by Colonel Abercrombie's light infantry.**

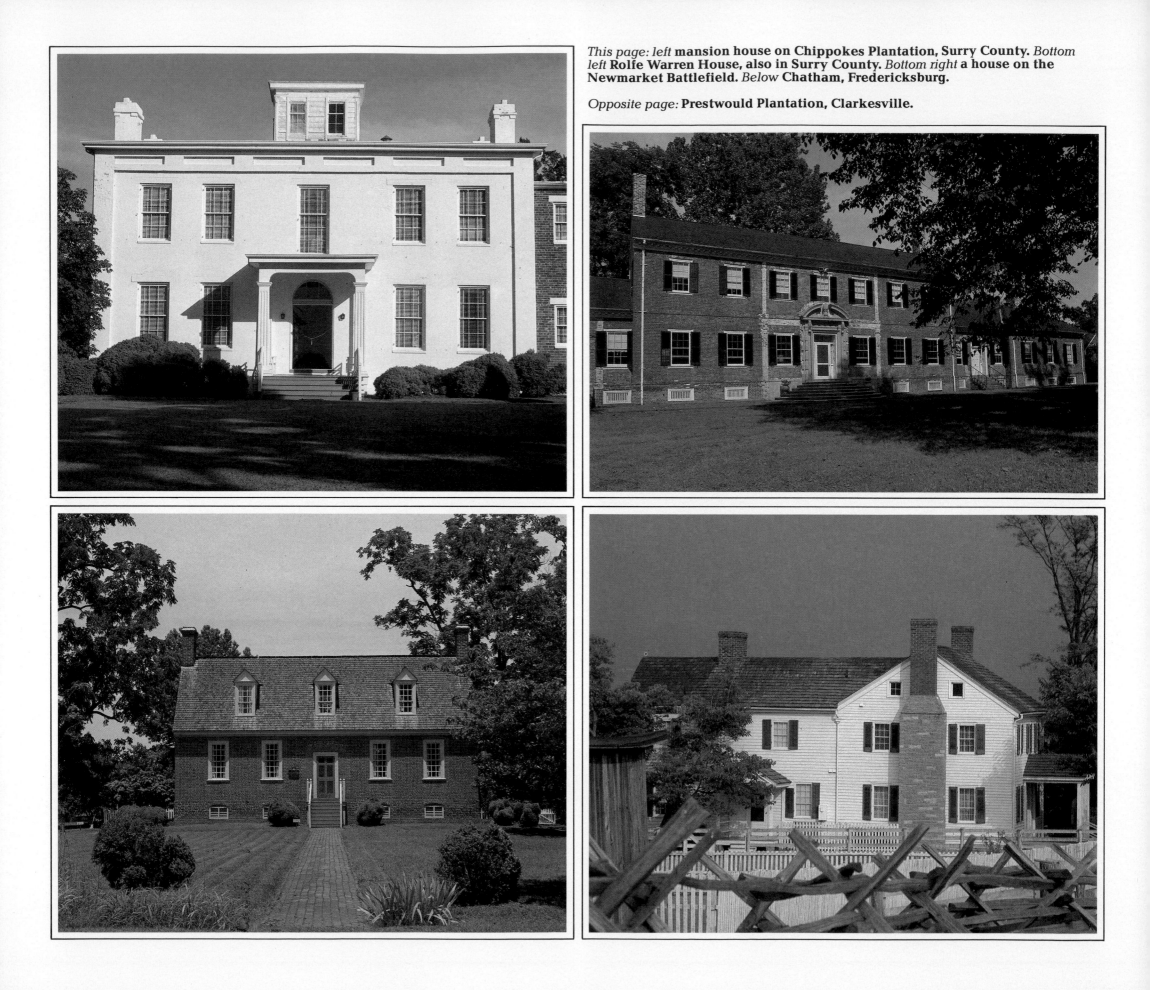

This page: left **mansion house on Chippokes Plantation, Surry County.** *Bottom left* **Rolfe Warren House, also in Surry County.** *Bottom right* **a house on the Newmarket Battlefield.** *Below* **Chatham, Fredericksburg.**

Opposite page: **Prestwould Plantation, Clarkesville.**

Opposite page: **the Norfolk riverfront and the marina.** *This page: far right and below* **scenes along the waterside of Norfolk.** *Bottom right* **Buckroe Beach and the pier. It has sand almost as fine as that of Virginia Beach and lovely waters, but its attraction is that it has a quieter charm.** *Right* **the First Landing Cross, on the beach at Cape Henry, is a granite memorial to the first English settlers in the New World. They sailed there in three tiny ships:** *Godspeed,* *Sarah Constant* **and** *Discovery.* **Landfall was made on April 26, 1607. These men eventually settled at Jamestown some thirteen years before the Pilgrim Fathers came to Plymouth Rock. As the colonists set back for their ships they were attacked by Indians, who wounded several of them. They replied successfully with their muskets and stayed to explore for several days, then put up the cross, which was then of wood.**

These pages: the sun's rays are reflected in a path of
gold from the waters of the Elizabeth River. Across
this river, from Norfolk, is Portsmouth which stands on
a water-locked point of land. It was established in
1752 and some of the 18th-century buildings survive.

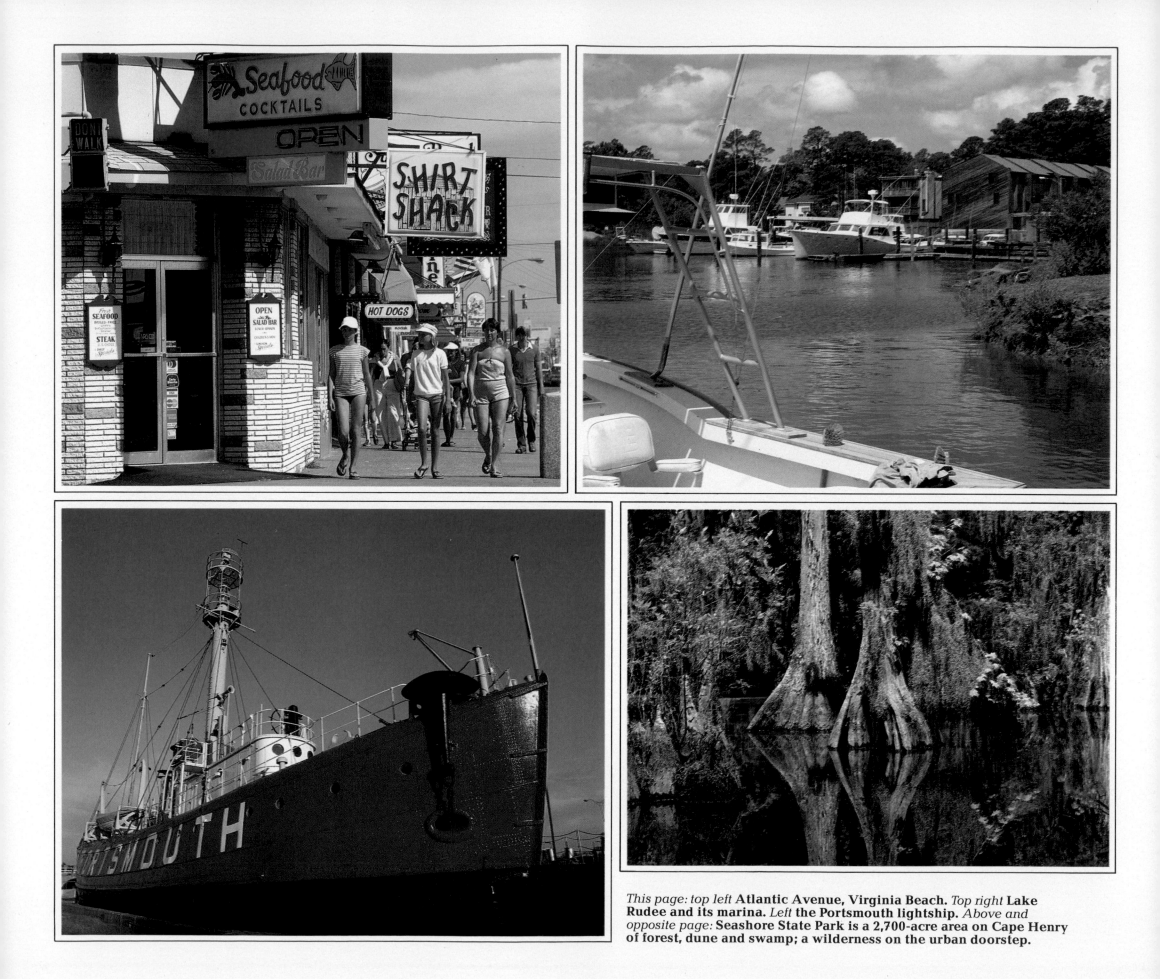

This page: top left **Atlantic Avenue, Virginia Beach.** *Top right* **Lake Rudee and its marina.** *Left* **the Portsmouth lightship.** *Above and opposite page:* **Seashore State Park is a 2,700-acre area on Cape Henry of forest, dune and swamp; a wilderness on the urban doorstep.**

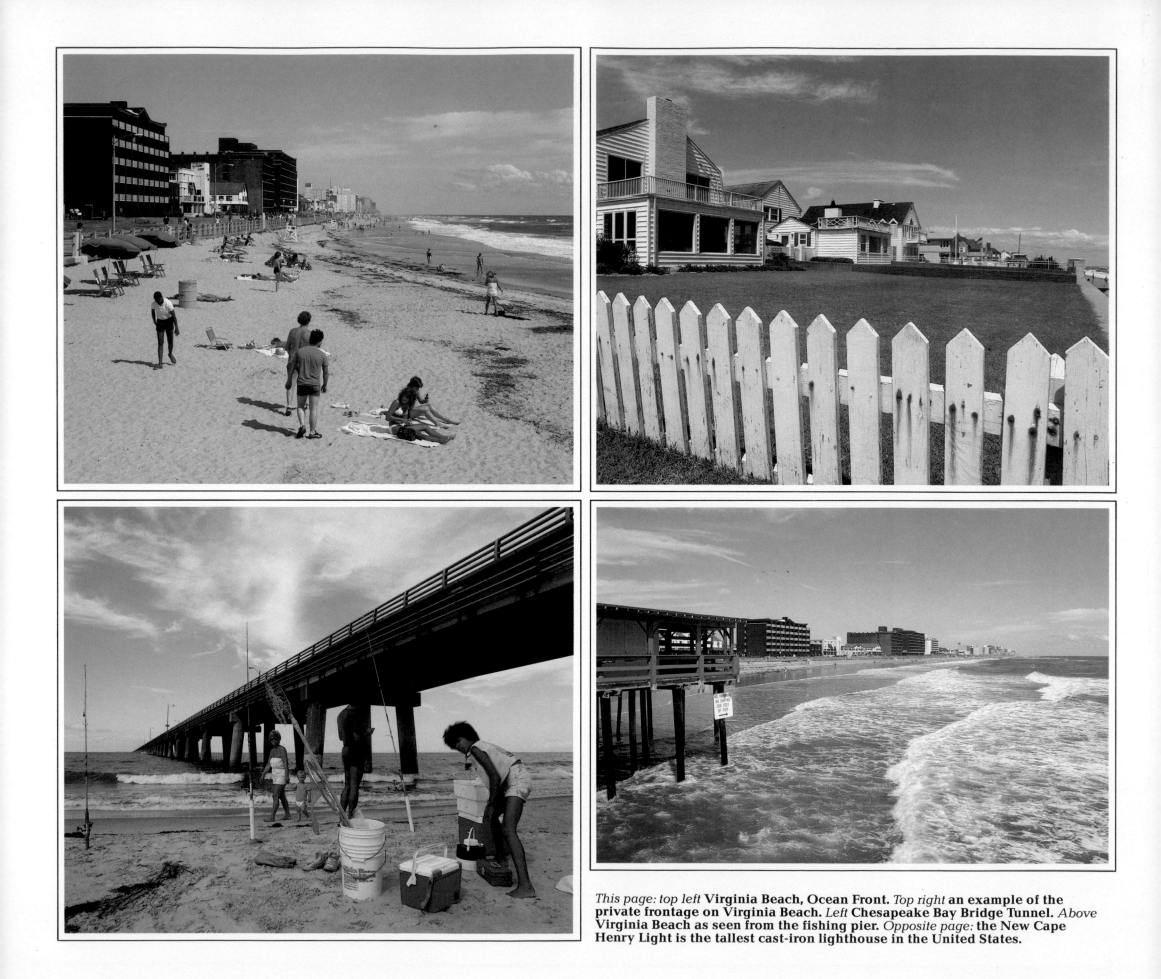

This page: top left **Virginia Beach, Ocean Front.** *Top right* **an example of the private frontage on Virginia Beach.** *Left* **Chesapeake Bay Bridge Tunnel.** *Above* **Virginia Beach as seen from the fishing pier.** *Opposite page:* **the New Cape Henry Light is the tallest cast-iron lighthouse in the United States.**

This page: **Buckroe Beach Pier.** *Opposite page:* **the fun of being at Virginia Beach. There are twenty-eight miles of fine, white sand beaches, which are washed by the waters of the Chesapeake Bay and the Atlantic Ocean.** *Overleaf:* **Chesapeake Bay and Beach.**

This page: **because of the warm Gulf Stream and the nutrient-laden Labrador Current, there is a wide range of game fish to catch. There are three piers that can be used, one on the Atlantic and two on the Bay.**
Opposite page: **a sunny day brings out the crowds.**

This page: *far left* **sunset silhouettes the spars and rigging of a boat on Chincoteague's waterfront and** *left* **mooring posts.** *Below* **daylight reveals a line of fishing boats riding at anchor.** *Bottom left* **Assateague Island as the last pale wash of sunlight gilds a path across the channel.**

Opposite page: **failing light silvers the waters along the Chincoteague waterfront.**

On Assateague are more than 250 species of birds. In summer there are nesting colonies of herons, ibises and egrets. In fall can be seen flocks of ducks and migrating hawks. Then in winter, flocks of swans and snow geese make their splendid appearance. Spring sees the arrival of oystercatchers, plovers, curlews and sandpipers. There are also the tiny Sika deer to be seen – barely three feet high – which were released there in 1923. Chincoteague is known for its shaggy ponies, which are a little larger than the Shetland breed. Traditional tales suggest that the first ponies swam to shore from a shipwreck in the 16th century, or that pirates had grazed them there.

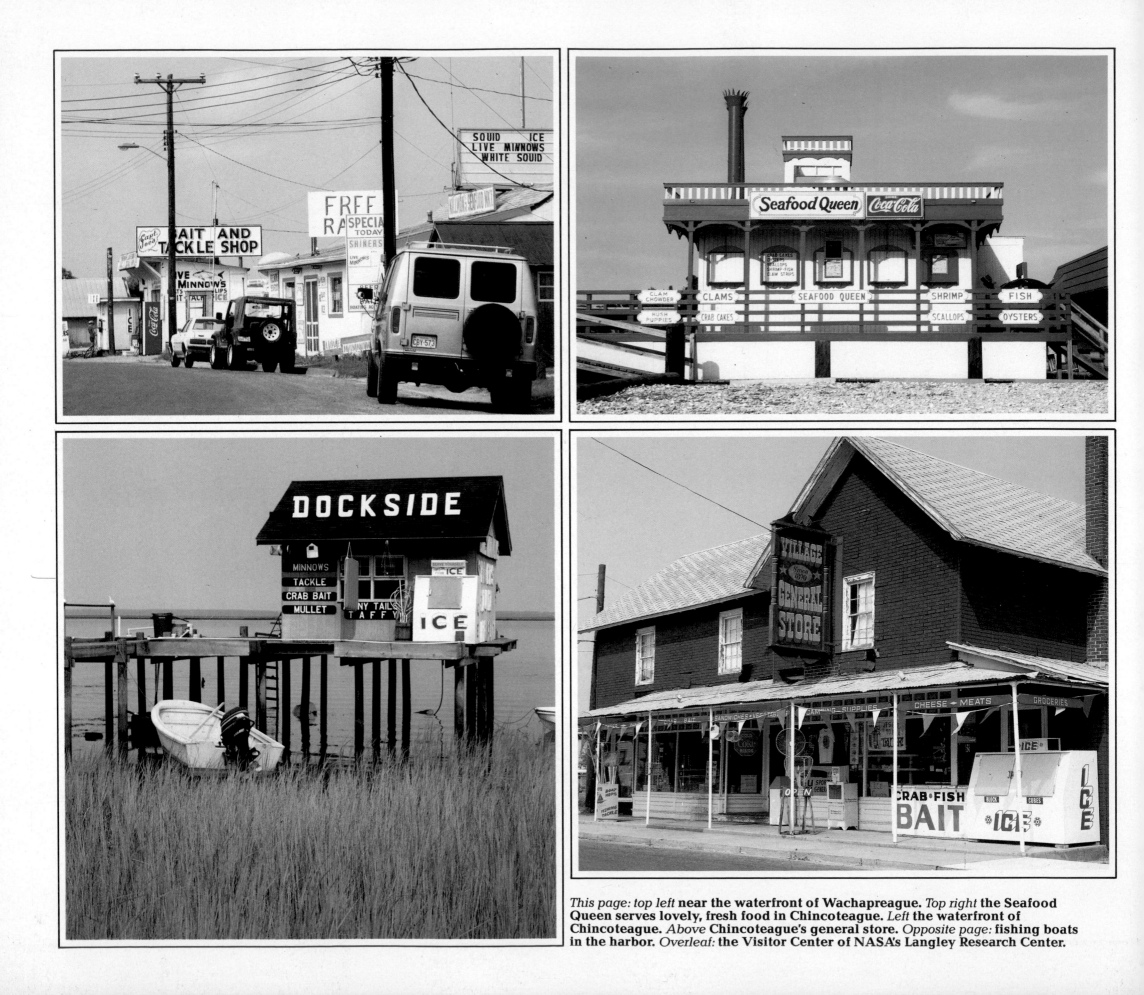

This page: top left **near the waterfront of Wachapreague.** *Top right* **the Seafood Queen serves lovely, fresh food in Chincoteague.** *Left* **the waterfront of Chincoteague.** *Above* **Chincoteague's general store.** *Opposite page:* **fishing boats in the harbor.** *Overleaf:* **the Visitor Center of NASA's Langley Research Center.**